The Bar Mitzvah Book

Advisory Editors	Eugene Borowitz
	Nachum L. Rabinovitch
	Louis I. Rabinowitz
Edited by	Moira Paterson
Contributions by	Isaac Babel
	Martin Buber
	Emanuel Feldman
	Gideon Fuks
	Uri Kaploun
	Jakov Lind
	Naftali Lowenthal
	Bernard Malamud
	Moishe Nadir
	Louis J. Peerless
	Bernard Reisman
	Isabella Rennie
	Jonathan Sacks
	Earl Shorris
	Henry Wasserman
	Naphtali Winter

The
Bar Mitzvah
Book

Praeger Publishers
NEW YORK

Published in the United States of America in 1975
by Praeger Publishers, Inc.
111 Fourth Avenue, New York, N.Y. 10003

© Rainbird Reference Books Ltd., 1975

This book was designed and produced by Rainbird Reference Books Ltd.,
Marble Arch House, 44 Edgware Road, London W2

House Editor: Peter Faure
Picture Researcher: Anne-Marie Erlich
Designer: Margaret Fraser

Text setting by BAS Printers Limited, Wallop, Hampshire, England
Printing and binding by Dai Nippon Co. Ltd., Tokyo

Library of Congress Cataloging in Publication Data

Paterson, Moira.
   The bar mitzvah book.

1.   Judaism—Addresses, essays, lectures.   I. Feldman, Emanuel,
1927–   II. Title.
BM42.P34   1975   296   74-20865

ISBN   0 275 33560 7

Printed in Japan

Contents

List of Color Plates

Except where otherwise stated the page number given is that opposite the color plate.

Acknowledgments

You, My Son, are the True King of Israel reprinted by permission of *The Antioch Review.*

Berestechko reprinted by permission of S. G. Phillips Inc./Publisher and Methuen & Co. Ltd from *The Collected Stories of Isaac Babel.*

Selected Yiddish Proverbs reprinted by permission of Schocken Books Inc. from *Yiddish Proverbs* edited by Hanan J. Ayalti, copyright © 1949 by Schocken Books Inc.

The Wrong Answer and *Drudgery* reprinted by permission of Schocken Books Inc. from *Tales of the Hasidim: The Early Masters* by Martin Buber, copyright © 1947 by Schocken Books Inc.

What does it Matter to You? reprinted by permission of Schocken Books Inc. from *Tales of the Hasidim: Later Masters* by Martin Buber, copyright © 1948 by Schocken Books Inc.

The Angel Levine printed with the permission of Farrar, Strauss and Giroux Inc. and Eyre Methuen Ltd from *The Magic Barrel and Other Stories* by Bernard Malamud, copyright © 1955, 1958 by Bernard Malamud.

At David's Tomb reprinted by permission of Jonathan Cape Ltd and Harper & Row, Publishers, Inc. from *The Trip to Jerusalem,* copyright © 1973 by Jakov Lind.

The Man Who Slept through the End of the World reprinted by permission of Andre Deutsch Ltd from *Treasury of Yiddish Stories* edited by Howe and Greenberg.

Introduction

We live in a fascinating time. On the one hand old and powerful nations have grown weary, western civilization is seized with ague and the glorious dreams of unending progress by advancing technology have turned into a sickening nightmare. With the terrifying threat of nuclear cataclysm never far beneath the level of consciousness, perplexity and paralysis have spread through many peoples.

On the other hand, new nations have emerged in the centre of historical awareness. With their goals set high they have plunged into a headlong race with disaster to achieve the 'greatness' which so long eluded them.

Meanwhile, the very globe is being emptied of its resources and famine and privation stalk the earth, making a mockery of the ambitions of the new nations no less than of the old.

In the midst of all this turmoil, there is one small people, at once ancient of days and newly-born. It is the bearer of a culture which is both the ripe fruit of millenia of development and the new flowering of the tree of life; at once burdened with the accumulated martyrdom of untold ages, still quaking in the throes of complete physical annihilation, and grown tall and vigorous with the sweet strong flood of hope coursing in its veins. The Jewish people is the enigma of history, the subject and the object of the most elusive of paradoxes.

Into this paradox a *bar mitzvah* emerges out of the innocence of childhood.

This book is meant to catch in words and pictures some facets of the fascinating reality that is the Jewish people. It is clearly impossible to compress into one book more than a glimpse of all the wisdom, all the sorrow, all the love and all the faith, all the struggle and all the yearning of the future as well as the past of this 'unique people on earth'.

By getting different authors to write about various aspects of the universal totality that is Jewish civilization, by combining fiction with exposition, poetry with history, art with photography, and other literary and artistic forms the book attempts to give young people some insight into the heritage and the promise that is theirs. Patchy though this attempt must necessarily be, if the book succeeds in evoking in the reader the mysterious throb of Jewish life then its purpose will have been amply achieved.

You, My Son, are the True King of Israel

We tested God from a hotel room overlooking Red Square. 'Come on, Lord,' I said, watching the summer lightning crack the sky over the Kremlin, 'come on.' Touch the red star with lightning, shatter the walls, give us a sign.

Rain fell heavily, swamping Marx Prospect. The five glowing red stars turned with the shifting of the wind. We counted the time between the flashes of lightning and the slow-travelling thunder, gauging God's aim. The new air of the storm washed away memories of the Augean stench of the Russian poor in summer.

'Destroy them, Lord, destroy them,' I said into the wind, mocking and longing for that old activist God of my forefathers.

'You sound like some kind of Southern preacher,' said my son.

'Joshua,' I muttered, not wanting him to hear, afraid that he would not know the reference. We had settled it all by then, but I did not want to recall the tears. In that room filled with creaking Victorian furniture, in that hotel sanctified by Lenin's brief residence in Room 107, at the corner of Marx Prospect and Bitter (Gorki) Street my son had become a Jew. I do not know what he lost there.

According to a survey made in the early 1950s by a Freudian scholar, people who had been atheists from childhood are less neurotic than those who have had God and lost Him. I no longer remember who made the survey, but it seemed as good a straw as any to one who became a father when he was still a child: God died before you were born, my son; I have said an empty *kaddish*, draped the mirrors, sat on orange crates; you are spared this mourning of abstractions.

We had gone north and east from Paris, a dubious radical and his thirteen-year-old son, two radicals on the Rive Gauche, that common comedy. M. Lévi-Strauss had fixed us with one eye and chuckled smugly over the aftermath of nuclear war. Hope is not a proper exception to the vision of an orderly mind. *Merci, Monsieur,* I will take that with me to Russia, though my luggage is already too heavy. But first we will go to a café beside the entrance to the Metro at San Michel to celebrate our inconsistencies with whatever they bring us when we ask for Coca-Cola.

It had rained, so we drank tea and sat under the awning. I wrote in a notebook: Lévi-Strauss' words, a description of his office in the Collège de France, reflections about his reflections on history, nothing of my awe or the good conversation I had failed to make. It had been a meagre visit; before the tea was cold I had closed the notebook, ending the visit but for the sound of his voice. He had said the word so softly, music for the cello: 'Doomed.'

We watched the street vendor, a Gallic hustler, we thought, so typical he should have been in the Michelin Guide-book. My son Tony went to buy a souvenir from him. They talked for a while, the vendor looking over at me and smiling during the transaction; such an intimate smile, I did not understand why. When he returned to the table I asked Tony what they had talked about.

'He asked me if I had been Bar Mitzvahed. Then he asked me if I'd been to Israel. He says he's been there, and he's going back.'

Discovery or revelation, there is always the same heat, the same speeding up; not guilt but nakedness: the Inquisition accuses, the Third Reich accuses, the Czar accuses, expelled from England, expelled from France, banished beyond the Pale, and now to be pushed into the sea. From the window of a tenement I saw them desecrating the synagogue, until the trucks arrived and the Jewish hoodlums recruited from poolrooms leaped out swinging baseball bats, a Stern Gang in Chicago in 1941, the defence of the Vilna *shul* under the street light. I was five years old. On the sidewalk where they fought I lagged filberts on holy days.

Discovery or revelation, the defences always rise: fists, though not for a long time; words now. Naked, I dress myself in words. Einstein, Nobel Prizes, violinists, cloaked in the Enlightenment, and before that the People of the Book, discoverers of God, the first to choose Him if not the ones He chose.

And that other defence: how does he know? Jews are an urban people; I have lived beside a cornfield; I have lived in a town without a *minyan.* Yes, I studied Hebrew, but so long ago. Now I know more words in the Dakota Indian language. Yes, I have heard Yiddish, but Spanish is my second language. Furthermore, I refuse to accept the judgment of a vendor of two-franc models of the Eiffel Tower; how could he have known? But he must have been sure. He would not have risked losing a sale. Is it because there are anti-Semitic slogans written on the walls of the Metro stops? France is an old country.

When we looked up, we could see him laughing, chattering away in French. He looked at us. 'You made the sale,' I thought. 'Look

OPPOSITE An entrance to the Metro

BELOW So we drank tea and sat under a café awning

LEFT The street vendor, a typical Gallic hustler

ABOVE The East Germans marching

BELOW Now there is a monument in the place where the Warsaw ghetto stood

OPPOSITE The ghetto fell fourteen years before he was born. What could he know of these people?

away. We did not come here for this.' The next day we left Paris.

Two years before, I had asked my son if he wanted a Bar Mitzvah or a trip when he was thirteen years old. He had said he wanted to visit Russia, and I had agreed to it. Some day he must also visit Turkey and Spain to find the tradition given to him by his mother. Now it was the Russian idea that fascinated him. He called himself a Marxist-Leninist without having read either. When he saw a booklet of anti-Semitic cartoons published in Russian newspapers and magazines, he said, 'The Russians have good cartoonists.'

We went to East Berlin to have a look at Marxism-Leninism there, and then by train to Warsaw, Bialystok, Vilna and Leningrad. The lesson of the street vendor continued. We saw the East German army marching, goose-stepping, slapping their boots on the pavement. Why was it funny in those newsreels? It is a dance step, elegant militarism, perversity. Yeats was wrong; there will be no slouching on the way to Jerusalem. We laughed because we were safe. In the melting pot anyone is an Aryan, everyone is pure because no one is pure.

There are no sleepers on the overnight train to Warsaw. We sat up, playing chess, talking to border guards, customs officials, and soldiers. At the Frankfurt on Oder station, the East German customs inspector stood outside our window, smiling, saying with his few words of English that he would like to visit America. And yes, he had heard of San Francisco. He stayed there outside the window until he had nothing more to say. And after that he stayed on, adjusting his red and grey cap, swinging his lunch pail. He was young, less than thirty. He had a wife and two children. During his off hours he went to some sort of technical school. He had never been to the West. He was not a Nazi, there had never been any Nazis. We stretched out on the seats and went to sleep. My son was safe. I had not seen the machine gun either.

There were three and a half million Jews in Poland in 1939. Now there is a monument in the place where the ghetto stood. The Polish women with kerchiefs hiding their hair and heavy boots hiding their legs, the thick women who push lawn mowers over the deep green grass around the other monuments of Warsaw are not needed at the monument to the forty thousand Jews who died resisting the Germans. The grass around the monument is brown and dry, there are dead stalks in the flower beds. The base of the monument is cracked. Polish children in short pants play war games there, holding on to the bas-relief leg of a defender of the Warsaw ghetto while leaning around a corner to pretend murder. Tony took pictures, and I stared at the monument and wept, not for the desecration of it, or for the forty thousand people who died during the weeks of resistance, but for those few who escaped the ghetto only to be murdered by members of the Polish Resistance.

I did not hide my tears from him, but I did not attempt to tell him why I wept. The ghetto fell fourteen years before he was born. There must be a limit to what we can mourn; we cannot make a Wailing Wall of the world. But later, in the hotel room I did tell him: Treblinka, Maidanek, house to house fighting, starving people against the army of the Reich. He listened, patient with me, attending a lecture in Warsaw on the Fourth of July; all history is the same, the lessons of the past are abstract, the calculus of culture. I reminded him to wash before dinner. He wrote a letter on Polish toilet paper. There was a floor show during dinner. We ate cucumber salad, veal and kasha. In the café before dinner we listened to Chopin and watched elegant whores sip vodka. Romantic Warsaw, resurrected in defiance of Hitler's promise that it would never rise again. Resurrected, all but the Jews.

I stepped into a ditch while running for the train at the Warsaw station, and turned my ankle. It swelled immediately. Tony had to help me to board the train. We went on to Russia, standing in line at Kuznica like refugees, walking through customs, dragging our luggage, sweating in the sun, surrounded by women in babushkas and boots, wicker baskets filled with bread and sausage. 'You are the descendant of refugees,' I told Tony. 'This is what it must have been like for them. One of my grandfathers walked from Moscow to Turkey, another bought his way out of the Russian Army. One of my grandmothers and her parents may have lived near here for a while, in Bialystok. They had come out of Bessarabia, leaving Kishinev, probably after the massacre. Later, we'll pass through Vilna, where one of my grandfathers lived.' He smiled at the thought of his Russian antecedents, considering Lithuania as Russia. When the train pulled in, he looked at the red star on the front of the engine. He was delighted. In a few minutes we would be inside Mother Russia; that was what he had come to see.

The train rolled past great forests and fallow flatlands. Poland had looked like Illinois before the invention of the tractor. The Russian countryside was even less efficiently used, intractable, even wild. The train stopped at Vilna. It was very late, but still light. In

Leningrad it would not get dark at all during that part of the summer. We looked out at the railroad station. An old Jew stood there, waiting, looking down the track, his hands clasping a book to his chest. He wore the wide-brimmed black hat, long beard and side-curls of the Hasidim. His face was stony, fierce, in search of the old, wrathful God of the prophets. The sky behind him was red. The light was wan, whitening his beard. He did not look at the passengers leaving the train, but kept his eyes fixed on the place where the track disappeared into the horizon, waiting. He must be mad, I thought. Did he expect the Messiah to arrive on the next train from Warsaw? The Hasidim are all slightly mad. Then it occurred to me – I don't know why – that he was waiting to go to Israel.

The conductor-porter brought us tea and sweet crackers before bed. Tony gave her a Kennedy half dollar and tried to tell her that he liked her, but he confused the verb with the preposition, and got only laughter for his painfully composed Russian declaration of friendship. After she left, he quickly fell into a deep sleep; it was nearly midnight, and we had awakened at five a.m. to catch the six o'clock train out of Warsaw. I lay awake a long time, watching him. My ankle, sprained at the train station in Warsaw, was swollen, discoloured and so painful I was unable to sleep.

In the darkness, listening to the sound of the train, cursing the Poles for putting a ditch down the centre of the railroad platform, I smoked Polish cigarettes, and sipped cold and bitter tea. I retrieved the old Jew at the railroad station to look at him more closely. He bore a strong resemblance to my great-grandfather, the one who had fled the 1903 massacre in Kishinev. It was from him that I had inherited the urge to be a writer. He was something like a rabbi, they said when I was a child. Later, there was a sort of confession: he had not been a rabbi at all. He had been a professional mourner, a frequenter of cemeteries who earned his living by crying over the graves of strangers: ten kopeks for a silent tear, a rouble for weeping, the tenth man at every *minyan* he attended. Did he earn enough money after the massacre to bring his family to America? Or had he been put out of work by the sudden spate of amateurs? Had he ever wept for a Russian who was not a Jew?

The old Jew fled, replaced by the faces of Russians; the border guards, customs inspectors, and the ugly, hairless man in the dining car. We had no common ancestors. 'Tony,' I said softly, careful not to wake him, 'you will discover one day that you are not descended from Russians, but from Jews who happened to live in Russia. And if you do have Russian blood, it entered the line when a Cossack fell on a Jewish woman and raped her. It's either history or racial memory, but I know it's true. This is not home.' And where is home? On his mother's side, Tony is descended from the Sheikh Sason ben Saleh, who is descended from Abraham Sason, the Venetian mystic who claimed to be a direct descendant

of Shephatiah, the fifth son of King David. I laughed aloud at the thought of travelling with royalty, and a Marxist-Leninist king at that!

We had been in Moscow for several days by Friday night. There was some tension between Tony and me. I was tired of the rudeness, intransigence and inefficiency of the Russians, and I hated them for their anti-Semitism. Tony remained fascinated. He did not mind that foreigners were barred from entering the public library or that they took an eleven per cent commission when cashing American Express Travellers' Cheques. He did not mind when the waitress brought out a great platter of quartered lemons when we asked for lemonade, nor was he upset to find water dripping from the ceiling in our hotel room. He mourned with them for their losses during World War II, and when he heard that the façades of the buildings on Gorki Street were made of red granite that Hitler had ordered from Finland for the monument that would mark his conquest of Moscow, he was proud.

We wrote letters, listened to the radio for a while, then got ready for bed. 'Let's set the alarm for seven tomorrow. I want to have breakfast before we go to the synagogue.'

'I don't want to go,' he said.

'Are you tired?'

'No.'

'Then why don't you want to go?'

'I'm not Jewish.'

'Of course you are; your parents are Jewish.'

'That doesn't make any difference,' he said. 'I'm free to be whatever I want.'

He sat on his bed, still dressed in his underwear, holding his pyjamas in his hand. His hair was mussed, curly, out of control as usual. The signs of adolescence were on his upper arms. Thick muscles were beginning to shape his arms and legs. Tufts of hair had recently appeared under his arms. My son, verging on manhood, bright and gentle, in many ways so strong.

We are barely a generation apart – twenty years and eight months. We are at war together against an insane world; is there no way for us not to be enemies as well as comrades? For a long time I did not answer. I am a slow-thinking man, easily surprised. I wanted him to be free as much as I want to be free myself. More. Being older I am responsible for increasing his freedom. But I had not succeeded, not for either of us. Rousseau was whispering to me: 'Man is born free; and everywhere he is in chains.' No, no, not free. Even that is a dream. Here was my own son demanding a freedom he could not have merely because he was my son. He was not even free to make himself safe.

Why was he afraid? Why was I afraid? Is the fear in our genes or do we believe history? Pogroms for me. For him the Inquisition too. My Jewish Heritage by Earl Shorris – a Bar Mitzvah speech. When I was thirteen years old I had spoken of a different heritage. I was not in Moscow. In the audience was a family of Polish Displaced Persons; they had lived in a cave for three years, eating roots and bugs to stay alive. I spoke to them of Moses, Hillel and Einstein. Tony could have delivered a more realistic speech.

We looked at each other, looked away, far from home, weary; it was not a confrontation that either of us wanted. Let him believe he is free, I thought. Let him feel safe even if it is only a dream. But that is the greatest danger, the real triumph of fear, the sickness that creates the docile victim.

Finally, I could do no more than tell him what I believed to be true. 'I wish you were free, Tony. But you can't escape. If you don't define yourself you'll be defined from outside. People have tried to escape it before, in Germany, in Spain. You know what happened.'

'But it's a religion, and I don't believe in it. So I'm not a Jew.' He began to cry: rage or fear or pain; it is impossible to know precisely the source of another person's tears.

'It's more than a religion.' I didn't know what to say. I hid in pomposity, talking about subcultures, about nothing, trying to smother the trouble in dulling words. Later, when we had returned to San Francisco, I would think about it, discovering myself in argument, arriving at advice for my son.

'I don't know the culture,' he said. 'I don't speak Hebrew or Yiddish. I don't even know the holidays. I'm free. I'm free to be whatever I want.' Tears fell from his eyes. Mucus distorted his voice. He clenched his fists, the hands too large for a child, but without the knuckles of a man.

How was I to define a Jew for him? Sartre's argument is the easiest, but Jews are not created by anti-Semitism. We are more. We are the eternal rebels, strangers who depend upon the hospitality of justice. We are the people of the book; our only roots are civilization itself. We are the history of the fallibility of man, the test of the goodness of nations, the invaluable victims by which judgment is rendered. We are wind and ashes; we cannot be destroyed.

It is not a history for children.

Nothing was resolved. His tears subsided. He changed into his pyjamas. We turned off the lights, and he went to sleep. After a while, I got up and walked over to his bed. I touched his temple. His hair, dark and curly and thick, as mine had been, as my father's had been before me, was damp, cooling him in sleep. In the morning I would go to face his fear.

There were fifty, perhaps seventy-five people in the synagogue. Most of them were old, shabby even on the Sabbath. But there was a light over the ark, and a rabbi with a great black and white

When the train pulled in, he looked at the red star on the front of the engine

OPPOSITE Gum, the main department store in Moscow

Most of them were old, shabby even on the Sabbath

beard, fierce as an Old Testament vision, sat in a high-backed chair beside the ark, staring out at the congregation while the cantor chanted the prayers for the Sabbath.

The beadle, a sleek, quick little man in a grey suit, gave me a *yarmulke* and a *siddur*, telling me several times that I must return the prayer book. I nodded that I understood – books in Hebrew are no longer printed in the Soviet Union. We spoke only a few other words: what part of America was I from? Had I been to Israel? It was forbidden for him to go to Israel. He was in a hurry; it is the nature of beadles. With quick little steps he led me to a chair in front of the first pew, opened the *siddur* to the proper page, then scurried up to tell the rabbi that there was an American in the synagogue. The rabbi and I exchanged smiles.

I spoke the perfunctory prayers, following the Hebrew text, mumbling responses in the tradition created by men for whom the words come like breath. When we stood for the silent prayer, I looked around me. They were faces I had already known: my uncle who left his business to spend his days with the Talmud, the old men of the Vilna *shul* rocking and bowing, body and soul in supplication, the grey hats in lieu of *yarmulkes*, the great noses, lined cheeks, frayed collars, arthritic hands, fouled consonants, tired eyes of the faithful.

I had abandoned them. It is twenty years since the marks of the phylacteries were on my arm, twenty years since I twice kissed my *tallit* and put it over my shoulders. I have derided them, my people, mocking my own soul. First a fearful child, then a cowardly man. I have shuddered at the sound of the word Jew, and it is my name.

There were no cowards in the synagogue that morning. I stood with defiant men who prayed not for mercy but for justice. Egypt, Babylon, Rome, Spain, Russia, Germany and now Russia again; we are like the despised insect that survived the ice age unchanged: we go on, while our grand enemies become history. We are few, but we are not meek, even in death. Our power is survival, life. The cantor sang the Ninety-first Psalm. His voice cracked, straining to the ancient melody. His song soared on the power of imminence:

> Thou shalt not be afraid of the terror by night,
> Nor of the arrow that flieth by day;
> Of the pestilence that walketh in darkness,
> Nor of the destruction that wasteth at noonday.
>
> A thousand may fall at thy side,
> And ten thousand at thy right hand;
> It shall not come nigh thee.

A Jew is an ancient and powerless man. In the Diaspora he learned that justice is the only shield of the minority and that the inheritance of the meek is the moral burden of man. Those were the lessons of the Inquisition, the pogroms and the concentration

Stone tablets from Babylon (top) and Sumer in the time of Abraham

camps. The lesson of the anti-Semitic intellectual was more subtle. The anti-Semite studied the Jew with great care, coming to the conclusion that Jews could not participate in modern society, a conclusion probably based upon empirical evidence, but not explained. The anti-Semite dabbled in notions about culture and religion, but could find no acceptable reason for the difference between Jews and Gentiles. The Jewish assimilationists denied the evidence, and instead of examining the anti-Semite's thesis, they pointed to his base motives.

Since the anti-Semite operates from a morally indefensible position, and his goal, which is to physically destroy the Jews, is so abhorrent, reasonable men have always joined the Jews in seeking to understand the motives of the anti-Semite while rejecting his thesis out of hand. It was unfortunate, for the anti-Semite appears to have been right: so long as the Jew remains a Jew, he cannot be an entirely modern man; he belongs in part to that time Rousseau called 'the youth of the world'.

Biblical Israel was one of the earlier societies we are generous enough to call civilizations. There is evidence in the earliest cuneiform writings of a people who may have been the first Hebrews. The existence of Abraham is suggested in an ancient mural. And there is little doubt that Moses was an historical figure. The Jews were among the first literate people, living in an area and under conditions that gave rise to writing and the accumulation of knowledge, the factors that distinguish modern from primitive societies.

The climate and geography of Mesopotamia, where writing first appeared, may have been more hospitable than that of Canaan, but the conditions must have been similar. The opportunity for men to own property, including slaves, and to set up hierarchies in which men had power over other men must have been nearly as great in Canaan as it was in the area between the Tigris and the Euphrates. Yet, something happened to the Hebrews, perhaps during their wanderings in the desert under the leadership of Moses, that caused them to fail to incorporate the primary concept of modern civilization into their culture. They adopted writing – the Law was inscribed on stone tablets – and other aspects of modern civilization, but they retained a primitive concept of the value of property, which was in direct opposition to the basic motivating force of the development of modern civilization – writing, the primary tool, was invented to catalogue property when the amounts exceeded the capacity of memory.

The evidence of the primitive nature of the Hebrew concept of property is most clear in a comparison of Hebrew and Mesopotamian Law. Hebrew law was thought to be the word of God. Therefore, the Law was immutable, and all men were equally bound by the Law. The Code of Hammurabi, by contrast, was the work of a man, who in his role as lawmaker was above the law. But

The code of Hammurabi, king of Babylon, inscribed on a pillar

more important, the Hebrew laws and the laws of the Hittites, Babylonians, Assyrians and other Near Eastern peoples differ greatly in their valuation of life compared to property.

Hebrew law was concerned with human rights above all others, while the laws of the neighbouring Near Eastern states were concerned mainly with the protection of property. In the case of theft, the law of several of the Near Eastern countries prescribed the death penalty, equating life with property. Hebrew law was archaic, primitive, refusing to join its neighbours in protecting property with the death penalty. And in the case of murder, the archaic nature of Hebrew law is proved again, for death can only be punished by death, a life for a life. In the neighbouring modern states, murder was punishable by the forfeiture of property.

The reverence for life, including the belief that the value of life is beyond equal, is impressive, but the lenient attitude toward offences against property in Hebrew law is astonishing. A modern concept of property is vital to the development of a modern state; it permits the expansionist policies that produce great nations; it allows lives to be lost in the quest for new property and increased power; it permits slavery, and it urges conquest and exploitation. The Hebrews, forged in their wanderings in the desert, a generation out of slavery, had neither property nor power to protect; they could acquire the results of modern civilization, but its basic motivations were necessarily alien to them.

Even after the Hebrews settled in Canaan, establishing vineyards, orchards, flocks and cities, they could not adjust to the modern concepts of power and property, for there is a primitive element in Hebrew law that makes such changes impossible: the law is not made by man, it is given by God; the law cannot be changed. It is the primitive concept of the completed world, the closed circle as opposed to the infinite line of modern man, and belief in the law is the first principle of Jewish life. The conclusion of the anti-Semite is a fair one, the Jew, as long as he remains a Jew, cannot fully participate in the modern world, for he is not entirely a modern man, but a hybrid, a primitive humanist outfitted with modern tools.

For the ancient state of Israel the failure of modernization promised disaster: the state had no philosophical basis for expansion of its territory or power; it was destined to remain small and vulnerable, to put prophets before kings. Conquest and exile were inevitable; primitive humanism could produce Isaiah and Christ but not Alexander or Caesar. Full entrance into the modern world was prohibited by the concept of the God-given law which could not be changed except perhaps by a Messiah, but a people used to living under a law that forced the equality of men by its God-given immutability could not easily accept any man as closer to God than all others. There was no avenue by which the Jew could escape his hybrid culture; he could write, learn science,

fly to the moon in a rocket, but as long as he believed in the Hebrew law he was part ghost.

Israel is a kingdom of the mind. Jerusalem is a metaphor, the promise of justice.

You are but one king among many; all Jews are equal before the ancient immutable law.

Though we are a hybrid people, we internalize history, and our history has made us afraid, limiting our freedom to be conquerors, restricting our capacity to rationalize evil. Being powerless and equal, we are the mirrors of each other, we are unable to escape guilt. Our only political passion is justice, making us gadflies by birth, putting us in constant danger.

It is an ancient and honourable tradition, but it is a difficult way to live. We can escape into Zionism or self-hatred. We can abandon ourselves to process or delude ourselves into security by joining our enemies. We can hide in blindness. Or we can remain part of the nation without a state, the arrogant meek, the wards of justice.

Those are the choices. Kings are free.

EARL SHORRIS

Israel is a kingdom of the mind.
Jerusalem is a metaphor

The Individual and the Community

Perhaps it is reasonable to regard the survival of the Jewish people as a miracle. What other explanation is there for the persistence, as a cohesive group, of a people without a home, always alien when not actively persecuted, driven from place to place for nearly two thousand years? But if it was a miracle, it was a down-to-earth one, firmly based in the people's determination to live as a community. A Jew does not exist in isolation. Through his membership of the Jewish community, he increases his individual satisfaction, and by his individual contribution, he increases the strength of the community.

Why did the Jewish people survive? Not because of its numbers, nor because of its power. It was never really numerous, nor ever powerful. It never ruled an empire. Many peoples, stronger and greater, have vanished, vast empires have disintegrated. Yet the Jewish people has survived. It continued to exist even when driven from its homeland and subsequently from many temporary homelands, when dispersed and persecuted. Not only did the Jewish people survive, but its spiritual values became the basis of the moral values of a great part of the world. The Bible became the world's most common book and the cultural heritage of ancient Israel that of Western culture, that same culture which spurned the Jews themselves. Despised, rejected and frequently attacked, the Jewish people has clung to its identity through the centuries. Wherein lies this strength? Just what does it mean to be a Jew?

The Jew as an Individual

The Jew reaches adulthood on his *bar mitzvah*. The very term defines the Jewish view of the meaning of this 'coming of age'. Literally he is now 'a son of the commandments' but, more correctly, the words mean 'liable to the commandments'. Before the *bar mitzvah*, a child is not required to keep any of the commandments which form the basis of Jewish life and thought. Only as a matter of education is he asked to conform to the ways of his parents and the community. Now, however, he is required to keep the commandments as a duty. He has entered the adult world where, as a Jew, a specific code of behaviour must govern his actions, actions which give him a great responsibility and for which he himself is now answerable.

The Jew reaches adulthood on his *bar mitzvah*. Celebrating the joyous event in Ein Kerem, a village near Jerusalem

25

What is not always clear is what, for an individual adult, these responsibilities really are, or why the ancient commandments should be the central motif of the behaviour of the Jew today. In order to clarify these questions it is necessary to define the individual, his personality, requirements and aspirations, and also the purpose and ultimate aims of the individual.

Every human being is composed of two basic parts, the material – the body – and the spiritual – the soul. Each of these makes its own demands and receives its own satisfaction. Often the two seem to be opposed to each other but in fact together they constitute the personality of the individual. Man, the Bible informs us, was created in the image of God (Gen. 1:27). This does not refer to the outward form of the human being, but his inner spirituality, his ability to think and feel and sense things, as well as his ability to give expression to his innermost self. It is this inner self which controls and gives life and personality to his outer form, and it is through his spiritual being that man differs from the animals. This spiritual being of man, which is his real self, cannot, however, develop freely, for it is subject to, and limited by, his other self, the body.

Both parts of the human being, the body as well as the spirit, need food for their growth and development, and each, if starved of food, becomes weak or withered. The body is developed by food and exercise. Any shortage is usually noticed quickly and remedied. Not so the spiritual. By its very nature the spiritual is less definable and its requirements less noticeable. The danger of the spiritual part becoming weakened is therefore much greater.

In order to prevent the decline of the spiritual in man and to further its development, certain schools of thought championed an approach which encouraged sole concentration on the spiritual to the exclusion of nearly all else. The material part of life was curtailed to the bare minimum required for survival. This is the withdrawal entailed in hermit or monastic life, where material attractions are not allowed to interfere with spiritual development.

This is not generally the Jewish attitude. Judaism does not demand the separation of the material from the spiritual; does not ask that a person should suppress his material needs and wishes. It does believe in integration of the material with the spiritual. Just as the body and the spirit constitute a single unit, opposed though they seem to be in their needs and desires, so also must the food for both parts constitute an integrated whole. If the body's demands alone are catered for, and only its hunger satisfied, then that hunger increases, growing with every temporary satiation. Alcohol, sex, drugs all follow the same course of addiction. On the other hand, if the body and the spirit are fed at the same time, the total personality grows. Man's personality is like a pair of scales which must be kept evenly balanced.

Balancing the spiritual evenly with the material is merely one

A model of the Second Temple

stage. The ideal of Judaism is much higher than this, for it sees in the creation of man a far more elevated purpose. It asks that man's material needs contain a spiritual content. It does not deny satisfaction to physical desires, but asks that they be satisfied on a spiritual basis and illuminated with spiritual meaning. Judaism recognizes that the body is the external form of the human being, and must be integrated into his personality by being unified with the spiritual self. In other words, Judaism demands a spiritualization of the material.

A Jew is required to participate fully in life, and his way of life is fashioned by free choice. He must learn to differentiate good from bad. Just as he will refuse to eat poison no matter how attractive its taste or form, so he has to learn to avoid those things which would cause him spiritual harm. Such actions as are negative, antispiritual, which appeal only to the baser instincts in man and accentuate his material nature, must be avoided. The normal material requirements of a person must be met, however, and these must be given an inner, spiritual meaning, and made into a spiritual experience. In developing his spiritual nature every material being gains a new significance. It becomes purified and spiritualized. The two parts of the human being become welded in a single aim and purpose and at the same time achieve a unity of personality and elevation of spirit.

Every action a person performs, even the most mundane, is

given an inner and wider meaning. There is no divorce from life but a sanctification of life and its actions. This is the meaning of the many commandments which a Jew has to keep. They dominate and pervade his everyday life and dictate his every action. Wherever he goes, whatever he does, he is surrounded by the *mitzvot*, the commandments. They do not allow him to forget himself, but teach him that his actions must have a fuller, spiritual meaning. They make even his material needs food for his spiritual being, without neglecting the material requirements of the body.

On the Sabbath, for instance, the Jew is commanded to take three meals. These are not merely an indulgence in good food and drink. They serve only to accentuate the difference between the Sabbath and the ordinary weekday. The careful preparations, the special food and the form given the meal, all help to make it a festive occasion. The lighted candles in the evening remind one of the holiness of the Sabbath; the *kiddush* over the wine at the beginning of the meal stresses the holiness of the day; the two loaves (*hallot*) signify Israel's reliance on God in the wilderness, where Israel was chosen as God's special people. Above all the meal provides the opportunity for discussion of the weekly Bible portion, for singing hymns of praise and for an inner relaxation and sanctification. The body receives its food but the experience is a spiritual one.

Similarly, other commandments which are outwardly material create an inner spiritual consciousness. The development of the spiritual and the transformation of the material into spiritual experiences give a different meaning to a Jew's life and enable his personality and individuality to find fulfilment on a higher plane.

The Jew and the Community

The individual cannot stand by himself. Whether he will or no, he is a part of the Jewish community. Just as physically a person often resembles his parents or grandparents so also is a person's character formed first and foremost by his family. Many characteristics are inherited, others are the result of his immediate surroundings. These are influenced in their turn by the community he lives in and, in a wider sense, by the nation to which he belongs.

A Jew, besides being an individual, is also a part of the Jewish community, which is itself a part of Judaism. The aim of the Jewish community is to unite and combine the activities of its individual members. It helps them to reach the goals they have set themselves and which they cannot reach alone. The most obvious example is the necessity for communal prayer, the *minyan*. Whereas the prayer of a single person can be powerful, it is much more powerful when said together with others, for then all the prayers combine, so to speak, into a single tenfold prayer.

No individual can reach absolute perfection on his own. He

The cantor at Gonda, Ethiopia

may, at the most, attain individual perfection, but this is not absolute. The rabbis point out that the difference between Noah and Abraham was that Noah was an individual saint – he was saintly in himself, and in his ways, but did not concern himself with others. Abraham, on the other hand, did not keep his virtues to himself, but extended his care to others. Their welfare, material and spiritual, was his primary concern. However important individual saintliness may be, the saintly community takes precedence over it. According to the Midrash all Jews, past, present and future generations, were present at Sinai when God made His covenant with Israel and chose them as His people. Each individual is therefore a unit in this community and only through the community can absolute perfection be attained. By the common fulfilment of the *mitzvot*, the community can raise itself up and reach a communal spirituality which in turn reflects back on each of its members. The individual working through the community and as an integral part of it, can attain

ABOVE A member of the ancient Jewish community of Kerala, India

LEFT In Djerba, an island off the coast of Tunisia, lives one of the oldest Jewish communities in the world. The hand and fish designs painted outside the woman's door, age-old Middle Eastern symbols, ward off evil and bring fertility

Before the Holocaust: Jewish builders in Lodz, Poland

that spirituality which exists only in the community as a whole, which belongs to it as a part of its essence as a 'kingdom of priests and a holy nation' (Exodus 19:6).

Each individual, however, holds the balance of the community in his hands. His every action is decisive, not only for himself but for the community as a whole. Every attainment on his part is an achievement belonging to the community, and any failure is not only his own but affects the community. Every member of the community, therefore, has a common responsibility. For the failure of the one is the failure of the other, and is the failure of the whole. And just as no Jew can ever renounce his Judaism – for a Jew despite all his sins remains a Jew – so also is he unable to give up his membership in the Jewish community, for despite every act, he still remains a part of the community. But although the community is affected by the actions of its individual members, as a unit it remains a whole, a unit in its own right, over and above the actions of the individual. The community is judged as a whole, not only by the merits of its individual members. It is complete in itself and its relationship to God is that of a single body, even though it is made up of many individuals. This relationship is therefore different, on a different scale and with different values, from the relationship of the individual to God. Both, however, stand in a direct relationship, the one on the individual plane and the other on the communal, national plane, and both must seek that spirituality which is the direct link with God.

Skin-workers in the ghetto in Cracow, Poland. Both Jews and ghetto were wiped out in World War II

Jewish Survival

Judaism believes in participation in life as a whole, but that participation must be sanctified. This is no easy task. Normally a person is so absorbed in his everyday life and career that he loses sight of the ultimate. His daily needs and social obligations are so demanding that he tends to ignore the higher, more spiritual values. Even the Sabbath, whose purpose is essentially spiritual, is frequently regarded as a social event and no more. So also on the communal-national level: the community is absorbed in its social life and functions while the nation has to face its daily problems and dangers. For the Jewish people, however, spiritual existence is its very essence. It cannot exist without it.

After they were driven from their land by the Romans, the Jews continued to survive as a people. The loss of their homeland did not destroy them as a nation. Everywhere Jews congregated in communities. Their national life continued and developed. Where possible the communities became autonomous, with their own institutions, their own law courts, and their own internal taxation. Great centres of Jewry sprang up outside Eretz Israel and often became important factors in the social and political life of the host country. Such was the case in Babylonia, in Spain and in Poland-Lithuania, to give but three outstanding examples. Central to Jewish communal life and Jewish identity was Jewish culture and Jewish learning. These were based on the Bible and the Talmud and on the observance of the commandments. The commandments were the national unifying bond that allowed a Jew to feel himself at home in any community. They were also mostly the yardstick by which the individual – or the community – was judged. Jewish learning and the adherence to the commandments were the key to Jewish autonomy and Jewish survival.

With the approach of the modern period the ties which had previously bound the Jewish people became weakened. Learning became in many cases the preserve of the few, in other cases it was turned into an intellectual exercise. It began to become divorced from the realities of life. On the other hand, the influence of the outer world, which had itself undergone great changes, began to penetrate Jewish consciousness and the Jewish world. Emerging national states did not favour the continuation of semi-autonomous minority states within their borders. These factors combined to change the Jewish communities in Europe, where by this time the majority of the Jewish people found itself. The new conditions called for new attitudes. One of these was given expression by the Haskalah movement, a movement which advocated integration into the culture of the host country. Although strongly Jewish at times and in certain places, it eventually meant that the Jew gradually lost his individual Jewishness and became absorbed in the life of the country in which he lived.

A completely different approach was advocated by a small but powerful group in eastern Europe, which spread and grew in numbers. These were the Hasidim, who sought the answer for Jewish survival in introversion, in strengthening Jewish life from within and anchoring it firmly round the figure of the saintly *zaddik*, the pious and learned central figure of each Hasidic group. (Most of the great Hasidic leaders were learned men, although the stress was on piety.) Other, smaller movements and groups emerged with time. The centre of Jewish life remained the Jewish community, and although large groups often broke away from the central organization to form their own, the community still remained the central feature, even if greatly weakened both in authority and in influence.

Together with these modern developments there emerged a third force, which sought a national solution for the Jewish people. Of this force the one seeking a Jewish national revival in the land of Israel (Zionism) proved the most enduring and successful. Through the efforts and example of individuals, who strove for the good of the many, the ancient homeland of the people was resettled. The movement gathered strength and many whose ties with the Jewish community had previously weakened found themselves enthusiastically taking part in rebuilding the national entity. With the emergence of a Jewish independent state, in its own ancient homeland, a new period began, calling for a reassessment of the role of the individual and the community.

OPPOSITE Slaying male infants, an Ethiopian picture of the persecution which led Moses' mother to hide him in the bullrushes so that his life would be spared

በቀተሌ ሄሮድስ ሕፃናተ፥

ራሔል እንዘ ተበኪ ሰደዊቃ፥

The Search for Perfection

When a baby is born it is helpless. Even its most basic needs are supplied and seen to by others. Slowly it develops. As it grows it takes care of its own essential requirements, and as the child reaches adulthood it becomes aware of the outside world, of others like itself and also of older adults whose world the developing child slowly grasps as he matures. The realization of the larger world creates a double drive in him: the desire to give free play to his own personality and the wish to create a better society as a whole. The two are not necessarily contradictory. As a person is not only an individual but also an integral part of society therefore the development, realization or fulfilment of his own personality will help the development and fulfilment of society as a whole. Since the greater the perfection of the individual, the greater the perfection of the larger unit, Judaism demands individual perfection as a step towards communal, national perfection.

An individual must begin with his immediate surroundings, which is himself. Paradoxically, self-perfection is achieved by being selfless, by working in the interests of others. By looking after his own interests, by catering to his own needs, he is actually stunting and debasing his own personality. So that developing his own self means in fact that he is also working for the good of others and in the framework of the community.

It is extremely difficult for a person to know at all times what to do and how to act. For this purpose Judaism supplies two guidelines: firstly, a fount of knowledge, given in the Bible, the Talmud and the Midrash (a most important and often neglected source). By intense and continual study of these sources the Jew arrives at a knowledge of Judaism and absorbs the spirit permeating it. By absorbing the spirit of Judaism a person is enabled to react in that same spirit and apply established principles to new and changing situations.

The basis for action is, therefore, knowledge and to attain this knowledge Judaism demands intense study. Every person must set aside at least part of his day for study. This principle of knowledge as the foundation for saintliness finds expression in the famous saying of the Rabbis, 'an ignorant person cannot be pious' (Avot 2:6). The second aid to a person's actions are the practical commandments which rule the life of the Jew. From morning till night his actions are regulated by the commandments, both those which concern himself vis-à-vis God, as well as those ruling his attitude and dealings with his fellows. The fact that he thus sets himself standards of behaviour also causes him automatically to strive for further perfection. He is constantly reminded of his duties which, if carried out in the correct attitude of mind, bring a person to the realization and fulfilment of his own self. His actions, whether laid down by the commandments or whether guided by his knowledge of Jewish

OPPOSITE The remains of a settlement at at Qumran, beside the Dead Sea, where a group like the Essenes lived in the first centuries C E

principles, have one common aim – the thought of God and the desire of closeness to Him. These two guidelines of Judaism help a person find direction and purpose. Knowledge and the practice of the commandments – and one is useless without the other – are only practical expressions of the guiding principle, which is the constant realization of God's presence. This is summed up in the Talmud (Makkot 24b) which declares that the essence of the commandments is 'the righteous shall live by his faith' (Habakkuk 2:4).

This then is the way to personal, individual, perfection. But the community, of which the individual is a vital part, must also reach perfection. In order to attain this communal perfection, Judaism includes a great number of communal commandments. The essence of the Jewish nation, which differentiates it from other nations, is its spirituality, its closeness to God, and the task of the individual is to help the nation attain this status. Because spirituality is so abstract it needs constant reinforcement, which must come from every individual working for the common good. Other nations, whose existence is bound by common material factors, do not need this reinforcement to such an extent, as the existence of material factors help to preserve the unity of the nation. Thus, for a nation whose

ABOVE Children in Birobidjan, a remote region on the Chinese border, which Soviet authorities still describe as the Jewish Autonomous Region. Founded in the 1930s as the Soviet answer to the 'Jewish problem', the 'National Home' in the USSR, it was never a success, and nowadays less than 9% of the population is Jewish

RIGHT Inside a synagogue in Venice, Italy

OPPOSITE ABOVE Grandfather blessing the bride in Vilna, USSR

OPPOSITE BELOW Jews from Bukhara (for centuries part of the Muslim world and now part of the USSR) celebrating *Simchat Torah* in Israel

An Oriental Jewish girl wearing her traditional headdress

nationality is bound by geographical borders reinforcement of national characteristics is not so vital, the geographical factors giving it a national unity, in addition to other national characteristics. The unifying bond of the Jewish people, however, is its spirituality, easily lost in the struggle for physical existence. There is, therefore, a vital necessity to reinforce this national essence on the individual, and national, scale. Any flaw, even that caused by the most insignificant individual, causes an imperfect state, not only in the individual but in the national body. Every person bears full responsibility for the state of the nation as a whole. This responsibility is not confined to himself. It also makes him responsible for the actions of others. The Rabbis therefore taught 'All Israel are responsible one for the other' (Talmud Bavli, Sanhedrin 27b), because the existence of the Jewish nation as a whole is affected by each individual's action.

The nation as a unit has, however, an advantage over the individual. For, whereas the failures of the individual are his own, and he is hard put to make them good, the failures of the individual in the national body can be made good by the deeds and qualities of his fellows. The imperfection of one is balanced by the perfection of the other. Every person has his good points at which he excels and thus makes up for the failure of others in that particular sphere. This is emphasized in the symbolic meaning of the four species used in the procession round the Torah scroll (originally around the altar in the Temple forecourt) on the festival of Tabernacles (Sukkot). The *etrog* (citron) has both taste and a pleasant odour; the *lulav* (palm branch) has only taste (the dates) but no odour; the myrtle has a pleasing fragrance but no taste; whereas the willow branches have neither taste nor odour. The taste represents the good material qualities and the fragrance the good spiritual qualities. All four species are held firmly together and if one of the species is missing the rest are useless. They represent the community and its individual members, who despite the failings of some remain nevertheless a single unit; yet each individual has his place and each is indispensable to the whole.

Attempts to attain not only individual but also communal perfection have persisted throughout Jewish history. In the time of the Second Temple the Essenes set up their own communities with special communal laws for a holier way of life, seeking the perfection of a Godly society. In mishnaic times we hear of a select group, the Haverim (comrades), with strict rules, especially in the sphere of ritual purity. In the Middle Ages, too, various groups at different times sought to find a way to communal perfection. One of the best known of these groups were the Hasidei Ashkenaz, in the twelfth and thirteenth centuries in southern Germany and the Rhineland, whose influence later spread as far as Poland-Lithuania in the east and Spain in the west.

Common to all these groups was a seeming paradox. They separated themselves from others by following strict rules made by the

group, for the group. They demanded rigorous adherence to these rules which differentiated their group from that of general Jewish society. The rules were regarded as binding on them only, as they accepted for themselves a higher moral responsibility. On the other hand they remained within Jewish society. Anyone was free to join, to accept their stricter mode of life, and their final aim was, in fact, to transform the whole of Jewish society. They were special groups but they remained within the framework of Jewish religio-national society. Their aim was to form a perfect community and from this, a perfect nation. The later Hasidic movement entailed a similar search for perfection.

The nation as a whole is a single unit and as such has a direct relationship with God. Although the actions of each individual add to or detract from the status as a whole, the nation as such retains its special relationship. Through this special status it also adds to the individual. For on the communal, national, basis its relationship to God is nearer than that of the individual, who by closer proximity and closer identification with the community or nation can thereby move to a closer relationship with God. For this reason, too, no Jew should separate himself from the community; in the well-known words of Hillel: 'Separate not thyself from the congregation' (Avot 2:4). By separating himself a person excludes himself from that closer relationship to God which he can only achieve as a member of the community.

NAPHTALI WINTER

No matter where their parents came from, these children play together in a Jerusalem alley

Moses at Sinai

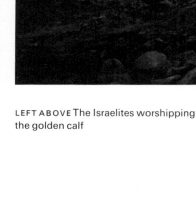

On the third new moon after the Israelites had gone forth from the land of Egypt, on that very day, they entered the wilderness of Sinai. Having journeyed from Rephidim, they entered the wilderness of Sinai and encamped in the wilderness. Israel encamped there in front of the mountain, and Moses went up to God. The LORD called to him from the mountain, saying, 'Thus shall you say to the house of Jacob and declare to the children of Israel: You have seen what I did to the Egyptians, how I bore you on eagles' wings and brought you to Me. Now then, if you will obey me faith-

The Wilderness of Sinai

fully and keep My covenant, you shall be My treasured possession among all the peoples. Indeed, all the earth is Mine, but you shall be to Me a kingdom of priests and a holy nation.'

On the third day, as morning dawned, there was thunder, and lightning, and a dense cloud upon the mountain, and a very loud blast of the horn; and all the people who were in the camp trembled. Moses led the people out of the camp towards God, and they took their places at the foot of the mountain.

Now Mount Sinai was all in smoke, for the LORD had come down upon it in fire; the smoke rose like the smoke of a kiln, and the whole mountain trembled violently. The blare of the horn grew louder and louder. As Moses spoke, God answered him in thunder. The LORD came down upon Mount Sinai, on the top of the mountain, and the LORD called Moses to the top of the mountain, and Moses went up.

And Moses went down to the people and spoke to them.

God spoke all these words, saying:
I am the LORD your God who brought you out of the land of Egypt, the house of bondage: You shall have no other gods beside Me.

You shall not make for yourself a sculptured image, or any likeness of what is in the heavens above, or on the earth below, or in the waters under the earth. You shall not bow down to them or serve them. For I the LORD your God am an impassioned God, visiting the guilt of the fathers upon the children, upon the third and fourth generation of those who reject Me, but showing kindness to the thousandth generation of those who love Me and keep My commandments.

You shall not swear falsely by the name of the LORD your God; for the LORD will not clear one who swears falsely by His name.

Remember the sabbath day and keep it holy. Six days you shall labour and do all your work, but the seventh day is a sabbath of the LORD your God: you shall not do any work – you, your son or daughter, your male or female slave, or your cattle, or the stranger who is within your settlements. For in six days the LORD made heaven and earth and the sea, and all that is in them, and he rested on the seventh day; therefore the LORD blessed the sabbath and hallowed it.

Honour your father and your mother, that you may long endure on the land which the LORD your God is giving you.

You shall not murder.

You shall not commit adultery.

You shall not steal.

You shall not bear false witness against your neighbour.

You shall not covet your neighbour's house; you shall not covet your neighbour's wife, or his male or female slave, or his ox, or his ass, or anything that is your neighbour's.

EXODUS 19: 1–6, 16–20, 25; 20:1–14

OPPOSITE When chasing Moses and the children of Israel as they escaped from Egypt, Pharaoh's soldiers drowned in the Red Sea

OVERLEAF An artist's vision of the Temple

The Law

The Jews are the people of the Book, but this same Book was later acknowledged as a source by Christians and Muslims. The Covenant God made with Moses, however, was the Covenant of the Law. Jews thereby became, supremely, the people of the Law. As Earl Shorris says in the first story in this book, 'all Jews are equal before the ancient immutable Law'. The Law has remained one of the cornerstones of Judaism. Its Interpretation has been disputed at times throughout history, but belief in the relevance of this God-given Law has been tenaciously preserved by Jewry against all odds.

What Sort of Law?

When we speak of Jewish law we do not mean the same sort of thing as, for example, U.S. law or British law. The law of a country lays down rules governing how a person must behave in respect of the society in which he lives; it regulates his conduct in matters concerning his relationships with his fellow-citizens. Jewish law is different. Although it does indeed concern itself with man's conduct vis-à-vis his fellows, it also deals with the relationship between man and God. Of course some important points in civil law do coincide with biblical commandments: we are forbidden to murder or to steal, but how we treat our parents, whether we are faithful to our husbands and wives, whether we envy our neighbours' goods, and, most of all, whatever sort of gods we worship – all these are left to the conscience of the individual concerned.

The notion that there are areas of conduct which can be left up to the individual conscience is a Christian one, in fact a specifically Protestant one. In Jewish law, the 'religious' and 'civil' elements cannot be separated. As we saw in the chapter on the community, Judaism recognizes no dichotomy between the spiritual and material needs of man, and in the same way Jewish law makes no distinction between the rules of conduct that govern the day-to-day actions of a man and his actions towards God.

For a Jew, therefore, the law is not something reserved for special occasions, such as solemn courtroom sessions and contacts with policemen. The Law of the Torah has something to say about how a Jew dresses himself in the morning, how and what he may eat, and how he should spend various festive seasons of the year. It teaches him how he should treat his wife, his children, his parents, his parents-in-law, elderly folk, strangers, princes and paupers.

OPPOSITE Moses with the tablets of the Law

41

BELOW A medieval painting of a child studying the law. Note the whip in the teacher's hand!

RIGHT Closer to reality: boys in a traditional *heder* forty years ago

Whether he is hiring or labouring, building or borrowing, he will find guidelines for his behaviour in the law.

So, too, Jewish law is not something a Jew can be 'against' in the same way that a citizen can be against a particular law in his country. It sometimes happens that good and law-abiding men and women will break the law in order to protest against some of the actions of their government. At other times, other good and law-abiding men and women wonder why the citizens of another country do not break its clearly evil laws. How far a citizen should follow the laws of his country when these laws are contrary to what he believes to be right is a very difficult question, which is indeed discussed in Jewish law. However, breaking one of the commandments of Jewish law cannot be a gesture of protest in this political sense.

Sources of the Law

The Hebrew word for the whole body of laws in Judaism is *halakhah*; a particular law is also called a *halakhah*, or a *din*. The former word comes from the root *halakh*, 'to go'. The Bible often speaks of the good life as the way in which men are 'to go'. In Exodus, for example, we read: 'and thou shalt show them the way in which they are to go and the deeds that they must do'. *Halakhah* is thus to be distinguished from *aggadah* – that part of rabbinic teaching which does not deal with laws, but which explains the passages in the Bible containing history and the moral teachings of the prophets.

The study of the *halakhah* has become the supreme religious duty. Indeed, the Rabbis said that since the destruction of the Temple, the Creator has nothing left in His world but the four cubits of the *halakhah*. This means that though the entire universe is His, the Creator feels most at home (as it were) in whatever nook *halakhah* is being studied.

The *halakhah* is in part handed down from Sinai, and in part derives from the teachings of the Rabbis.

The Written Law

Six hundred and thirteen commandments were revealed at Sinai and written in the Torah, the Five Books of Moses. Two hundred and forty eight of them are positive (*do's* – such as 'Honour thy father and thy mother'); the other 365 are negative commandments (*don't's* – such as 'Thou shalt not bear false witness').

Some of them are obligations between man and man, some between man and his Creator, and others are in evidence or remembrance of an idea or a historic event. Some regulate justice and righteousness in the community; others set out the private duties of the individual. Many of these laws have been borrowed

The destruction of the Second Temple. Titus's arch in Rome shows the Roman soldiers bearing off the spoils

and adopted (after the lapse of some centuries) by the nations of the world (see below). In this manner the People of the Book has indeed become (in the words of the prophet Isaiah) 'a light to the nations'.

Statements Handed Down by Tradition

These include the commandments which appear not in the Five Books of Moses (the Pentateuch), but in one of the other two sections of the Bible – the Prophets, or the later Writings (the Hagiographa), and which were received by the prophets either as interpretations of statements already appearing in the Written Law, or else as *halakhah* given to Moses at Sinai.

The Oral Law

This comprises three sources of Law: the interpretation of the Law revealed at Sinai; *halakhah* given to Moses at Sinai; and logical deduction.

1. Interpretation of the Written Law

There are certain verses in the Five Books of Moses whose interpretations were handed down at Sinai. These statements are always regarded in the Talmud as having the same force as if they actually appeared in the Written Law. In other cases, the interpretations are hinted at in the written word, whose meaning comes

OPPOSITE Head and arm *tefillin* in place (centre figure) during a *bar mitzvah* celebration

BELOW A bag made in Morocco to carry the *tefillin*

to light only through the use of the accepted talmudic rules for deriving detailed laws from scriptual verses. Some of these interpretations are regarded as being of rabbinic authority only.

2. ' Halakhah' given to Moses at Sinai

There are some seventy laws which have biblical authority, even though they have little or no mention in Scripture. An example which involves someone approaching *bar mitzvah* concerns the *tefillin*. From the age of thirteen, the *tefillin* are worn during the morning prayers. They consist of two small black leather boxes containing tiny parchment scrolls inscribed by hand with certain quotations from Scripture. One such capsule is placed just above the forehead, and the other on the upper arm. Scripture states in general terms that certain biblical passages are to be bound as a sign on the arm and between the eyes; the details of how this instruction is to be fulfilled have been handed down by tradition from earliest times. Thus the Talmud teaches that the requirement that the *tefillin* be square, that their straps be black, and that the tiny scrolls be written on parchment, are laws given to Moses at Sinai.

3. Logic

In the case of certain laws (*halakhot*), the authors of the Talmud do not seek a scriptural verse or an oral tradition as the source from which they may have been derived. Instead, they may say: 'it is self-evident', and thus needs no proof from Scripture. An example is the rule: 'If someone claims something which another person has in his possession, it is the claimant who is obliged to bring proof of ownership.'

Statements of the Scribes

These include the ideas derived in principle from the Torah and explained by the sages (as discussed above), as well as actual laws which they enacted. The Torah itself empowers the leading scholarly rabbis and judges of each generation to do this when it states: 'According to the law which they shall teach thee . . . thou shalt not turn aside from the sentence which they shall declare unto thee, to the right hand, nor to the left.' This refers not only to the scholars' interpretations of the text of the Torah, but also to any rule which they find necessary to make. According to the Talmud, the sages even have the power to abolish a biblical regulation in certain circumstances, or to disregard a biblical rule for a limited time, in order to reinforce observance.

There are of course limits placed on this legislative power. Thus, the sages may not impose a restriction on the community if the majority cannot abide by it. Nor may a court override the decision of another court unless it be greater in wisdom and in number – and it is exceedingly difficult to find an example of a rabbinical court in history that was prepared to arrogate to itself this status.

The sages assumed that no one would be careless with the observance of commandments (*mitzvot*) actually written in the Torah.

The customs of this Hasidic boy are very different from those of the Israeli soldiers who gaze at him in some wonderment

OPPOSITE Prayers in Elijah's cave, Mt Carmel, Israel

This might not be the case with their own regulations (*takkanot*). Accordingly, they sometimes made the observance of their regulations a stricter matter than the observance of the *mitzvot* explicitly stated in the Torah. Many of the existing *takkanot*, like much of the early *halakhah*, are anonymous. Some edicts, however, bear the names of particular persons or places, such as those of Johanan ben Zakkai, or the scholars of Usha in Lower Galilee.

Custom

A goodly portion of our life is regulated by custom (in Hebrew, *minhag*), which over the centuries has grown among well-informed Jewish communities around the world, and which has in the course of time been approved by the rabbis, until it enjoys the full force of the law. Thus the Jerusalem Talmud says: 'Whenever a *halakhah* is unclear in the *bet din* (rabbinical court) and you do not know its nature, go and see how the community conducts itself and act accordingly.' This is what Hillel meant when he once said: 'This particular *halakhah* I have heard, but forgotten; but leave it to Israel: if they are not prophets, they are the children of prophets.'

A classic instance of the recognized power of custom is the practice among observant Orthodox Jewish menfolk of covering the head. In Scripture there is no mention of it. The Talmud does discuss it casually, but it is custom – widespread and long established – that has given it its present status.

The strength of custom can best be seen by the cases where it contradicts the theoretical *halakhah*. Examples are to be found in the Talmud of religious, social or legal customs which were current only within a certain group – such as the citizens of a town, a fraternity of pious men, the womenfolk of a particular region, or a professional group – and which yet overrode the theoretical law. One such example is the case of the desert caravan which is hijacked by bandits. Talmudic law lays it down that when the bandits demand a ransom for the release of the travellers, each must pay according to the amount of property he carries rather than a fixed sum per head. However, 'the custom of caravan travellers (even if it differs from this law) must not be departed from.' In later years, especially in the Middle Ages when travellers were frequently seized by bandits or pirates and held to ransom as an alternative to being sold into slavery, it was the whole community which raised the ransom money for Jewish captives.

No custom, of course, can render permissible that which is clearly prohibited, although the opposite can happen. Certain customs were opposed by the sages because they were based on ignorance, or because they imposed unnecessary hardship on the public. In the talmudic period, for example, the fishermen of Tiberias were accustomed not to work on *hol ha-mo'ed* (the intermediate semi-holy days of certain festivals). The sages objected to this custom, since it would make it impossible to prepare fish for

the festive meals, and would thus detract from the joy of the remaining days of the festival.

Likewise, a custom must not conflict with the principles of justice and fair play. If, for example, it had been customary in some community to tax the rich and the poor equally, this taxation was deemed illegal; 'for certainly', as one scholar wrote, 'according to the law of the Torah taxes must be shared according to financial means, and there can be no greater injustice than to make the rich and the poor bear the tax burden in virtually equal measure; and even if the custom has been in existence over a long period, it must not be upheld.'

The above, then, are the main sources – divine and mortal, written and oral, formal and informal – of the Jewish law.

How the Law is kept up to date

In the Bible, a commandment is expressed in a few short sentences in Hebrew. Jewish scholars have always recognized that, as well as being eternal, a law is expressed in terms which apply to a specific time, place and set of circumstances and must be reinterpreted to apply to other times, places and circumstances.

After the destruction of the Second Temple by the Romans in 70 CE it became particularly important to reassess the law in the light of the greatly changed circumstances – the temple destroyed and many of the people exiled. The scholars who engaged in this task were known as *tannaim*, and among the most celebrated were Hillel and Shammai, Rabbi Simeon, Rabbi Meir and Rabbi Akiva. Their debates on the laws they received from their teachers are recorded in a compilation known as the Mishnah. At the end of the second century CE, Rabbi Judah ha-Nasi edited the Mishnah, and after the Bible it ranks as Judaism's most sacred text.

From the third to the fifth century, by which time Babylonia (now Iraq) had displaced the land of Israel as the main Jewish centre, though spiritual activity still continued there, the later scholars, called *amoraim*, had lively discussions of the Mishnah as taught by the *tannaim*. The result of their discussions, in which they included their not infrequent disagreements, were gathered together into the Talmud, which exists in two versions, the Babylonian Talmud and the Jerusalem Talmud. The Talmud, then, is a record of discussions held on different subjects, in different places, at different times. The explanations written by later commentators, especially Rashi, are printed alongside the relevant passages. But the Talmud is not a ready reference book. To make it easier to find the law on a particular subject, certain early legal decision-makers (*posekim*) attempted to codify the law. One of them was Maimonides in the twelfth century. First he wrote his *Commentary on the Mishnah*, the concluding passage of which points

OPPOSITE Safed, in northern Galilee, one of the main mystic centres in the land of Israel

OPPOSITE The cases containing the Torah scroll are often beautifully decorated. The centre one is a particularly magnificent example from 18th-century India; the one on the right from 18th-century Persia

out that the work was done 'in exile and in wandering from one end of the earth to the other, parts of it during journeys on land, others while voyaging in ships at sea'. Then in 1180 he completed the mammoth task of sifting through the whole mass of law as it had developed up to his day, extracting from each talmudic and rabbinic discussion those parts which had to do with each classifiable legal topic. He then grouped those topics into chapters according to their subject matter. The resultant fourteen-volume work, the *Mishneh Torah*, gave the final decisions up to that date on all questions of *halakhah*.

Whereas Maimonides mainly followed the halakhic opinions of the Spanish rabbis, the scholars of France and Germany often had differing views. These were recorded by other codifiers, such as Rabbi Asher ben Jehiel (known as the Rosh) and his son, Rabbi Jacob ben Asher, in the fourteenth century, whose four-part code is known as the *Tur* (for *Arba'ah Turim*, meaning the 'Four Rows').

Among the Jews expelled from Spain in 1492 was a four-year-old refugee by the name of Joseph Caro. Growing up to be a scholar in Safed, in northern Israel, he realized that 'the Torah was becoming many *torot*', because with the differing codes, different communities were understanding the law in a variety of ways. He therefore summarized the legal decisions of the majority of the preceding codifiers. In the Talmud, to be sure, the nourishment was all available – but only in its raw state. Caro prepared it and served it up ready for consumption, giving his work the title of *Shulchan Arukh*, 'The Set Table'. This work was first printed in Venice in 1565.

Caro's Spanish (Sephardi) origins, however, naturally gave emphasis to Spanish decisions, which did not always reflect the customs and practices of German and Polish (or Ashkenazi) communities. Understandably enough, they felt that something was missing to make Caro's 'Table' a little more inviting. Notes giving the corresponding German-Polish practices wherever they differed, were therefore added to the *Shulchan Arukh* by Caro's contemporary, Moses Isserles of Cracow, Poland. This work was aptly called the *Mappah*, which means 'The Tablecloth'.

Since then, the world has greatly changed. For example, electric lights and motor vehicles were unknown when Rav Ashi began editing the Talmud in the fifth century, as they were unknown in Moses Isserles' day, the sixteenth century. Does the law against kindling a fire on the Sabbath apply to the former, and the prohibition on travelling by horse-drawn vehicles to the latter? As each new invention made its appearance, the problem was tackled. The first task of the leading halakhic experts was to familiarize themselves with its workings. They then sifted through the existing body of law in order to extract its underlying principles, and they then decided on the question as to which basic rule of the *halakhah* the new invention should be classified under.

ABOVE The synagogue named for Joseph Caro in Safed, where he lived

ABOVE RIGHT The frontispiece of the first printed edition of Joseph Caro's *Shulchan Arukh*

RIGHT Guarding the Law. An Orthodox Jew watches anxiously as excavations begin by the side of the Western Wall

OPPOSITE ABOVE Bargaining in Tel Aviv for the *lulav* and *etrog* (palm branch and citron), essential components of Sukkot celebrations

OPPOSITE BELOW Purim, the festival celebrating Esther's deliverance of the Jews, is especially popular with children, who treat adults to gentle mockery in their fancy dress

It is obvious from this that the heritage of Jewish law – a development which took place over many centuries in many widely differing lands and societies – cannot be grasped in a short study. To master it is indeed a formidable task. But in the words of Rabbi Tarfon, the Mishnaic sage: 'You are not obliged to complete the task – but neither are you free to desist from it altogether!'

There are still desert caravans today, though no-one now hijacks these Beduin in Sinai

Jewish Law in the Wider World

Since the Jewish people lacked independence in a political sense for a long period of their history, and most of them lived and still live under non-Jewish governments, it is obvious that the scholars had to find some way to cope with the problem of the relationship between their law and that of the country in which they lived. As the prime source of Jewish law is the Bible, that is divine revelation, it must of necessity survive and the judicial autonomy of the Jewish people be preserved wherever they lived. But it was also necessary, for their continued survival if for nothing else, that the Jews be law-abiding members of their host society. To cope with this problem, the *amora* Samuel laid it down around 241 CE that *dina de-malkhuta dina*, the law of the land is binding in civil legislation. In some cases, these laws did not agree with the ruling of Jewish law on that particular subject.

Dina de-malkhuta dina therefore does not apply to every aspect of Jewish law. In particular religious and ritual observances are of course exempt. Whatever the law of the land, in matters of religion a Jew follows Jewish law. He is therefore bound to resist any government which tries to outlaw Judaism. It is only in civil matters that he must obey the law of the country in which he lives. To what extent he should do so was disputed by different scholars in different

OPPOSITE This old Cairo street probably looked much the same when Maimonides lived in the city

Children also enjoy *Tu bi-Shvat* (like Sukkot) an essentially agricultural festival

places. All believed that a Jew must obey laws which were 'in the ruler's interest', that is laws concerning the relationship between a citizen and the governing authority. Some scholars, however, did not agree that *dina de-malkhuta dina* applied to laws which related to private concerns between Jewish citizens. It was also agreed that the principle did not hold in the case of a law which distinguished between one citizen and another, though in the face of the reality of discrimination against Jews, the scholars were forced to limit this to laws which distinguished between one Jew and another.

In point of fact, until the emancipation of the Jews in Christian lands beginning in the early nineteenth century, in most matters concerning their day-to-day lives Jewish communities lived under Jewish law. Although the hand of the ruler sometimes fell heavily on them (especially as far as taxes were concerned), and although periodically their neighbours persecuted them, in peaceful periods the Jews lived in their communities free to follow the rulings of their own scholars. With the growth of the belief in equality for all, the Jews in Christian countries lost their previous autonomy within their own communities, although they gained by the fact that the law of the land ceased to discriminate against them. In Islamic countries, however, this was not so. There were only relatively few periods when Islam discriminated against Judaism with the same ferocity as Christianity, and the right of religious minorities to a separate (albeit inferior) existence is a recognized tenet of Islam. Until the break up of the Ottoman empire at the end of World War I (1918), the Jewish communities in Turkey, North Africa and all the Arab lands continued to exercise Jewish law amongst themselves. After 1918 the influence of Britain and France made many changes, not the least of these being the growth of nationalism, although in Arab countries the Jewish communities retained some degree of autonomy.

Whether directly or indirectly, many aspects of Jewish law later, much later, became law in other systems. Most important of these are some of the laws applying to women and children and to workers. Judaism entailed a system of 'social security' long before the concept became general in other societies. For example, under Jewish law the education of children is the duty of the whole community and orphans must be provided for out of community funds. In Jewish marriage, both husband and wife have rights and duties, deriving from law and not simply from agreement between the parties. From talmudic times it was laid down that a Jewish wife must be supported and clothed, cared for in illness, and provided for, in her own house, after her husband's death. These principles held good in a world where, for many centuries, a wife was regarded as her husband's possession. Neither a girl nor a boy can, under Jewish law, be married before maturity nor against their will. If a woman is divorced, her husband must provide her with the sum of money specified in their marriage document (*ketubbah*). Divorce is considered regrettable, but a couple is not condemned to live together in misery when it is clear to the rabbinical authorities that the marriage has broken down. All these things seem obvious to us now, but not so many years ago among non-Jews children could be married off in infancy to whomever their parents chose. Likewise, a husband was free to make his wife as miserable as he pleased and she was still compelled to go on living with him.

In labour relations too Jewish law was centuries ahead of the rest of the world. We tend to think that such things as regulated working hours, stipulated wages and severance pay on dismissal are the result of the rise of labour unions in the nineteenth century. And so in the larger world they are, but not in Jewish communities. Gross exploitation of the working classes is impossible under Jewish law.

From all this it is clear that, far from being a quaint fossil which has survived in the modern world, Jewish law has anticipated some of our most treasured modern ideas by many centuries. As it has evolved over the years, Jewish law has been continuously reinterpreted to adapt it to changing times and places, but its central core has been an unchanging rock on which the Jewish people built their stability and continued existence.

URI KAPLOUN

What Does it Matter to You?

A Hasid came to the rabbi of Kotzk. 'Rabbi,' he complained, 'I keep brooding and brooding, and don't seem to be able to stop.'
'What do you brood about?' asked the rabbi.
'I keep brooding about whether there really is a judgment and a judge.'
'What does it matter to you?'
'Rabbi! If there is no judgement and no judge, then what does all creation mean?'
'What does that matter to you?'
'Rabbi! If there is no judgement and no judge, then what do the words of the Torah mean?'
'What does that matter to you?'
'Rabbi! "What does it matter to me?" What does the rabbi think? What else could matter to me?'
'Well, if it matters to you as much as all that,' said the rabbi of Kotzk, 'then you are a good Jew after all — and it is quite all right for a good Jew to brood: nothing can go wrong with him.'

MENAHEM MENDEL OF KOTZK collected by Martin Buber

The Family

In the chapters on the Law and membership of the Jewish community,
the writers show how central it is to Judaism that the Jew does not turn
aside from life in this world, but embraces it within the Jewish context.
To live a true Jewish life is to love life, and to love life is to love God.
The love of God is shown in and through a person by his capacity to love
his fellows. In Judaism this love is learned first of all through the family and
is demonstrated by it. In the family the love of man and woman attains its
full physical and spiritual expression; the two halves of humanity are
completed in this bond. So, too, the family is where a child first learns
about love, and by means of the love between himself and his parents and
between his brothers and sisters experiences the love which he will later
extend to others. At first, his family is a child's whole world, and in it
are laid the foundations of his ability to live fully and to love truly.

Judaism is an old and complex religion. In some of the other
chapters its rich history and varied customs are outlined. However,
when I think about what it means to be a Jew and what my *bar
mitzvah* meant to me, most of my thoughts go back to scenes from
my life with my family. I remember the small personal events that
somehow made me the man I am today; not just any man, but a Jew.

There are already so many excellent guides to the life of the individual Jew and the cycle of the Jewish calendar that I decided to
take a different approach. I want to recall a few of my own more
personal memories to suggest how I felt at different points about
these two abstract cycles. Of course, these memories will not be
shared by everyone reading this book, but they do suggest some of
the many possibilities that are created by the Jewish family.

I remember the excitement around our house as Sabbath was
approaching. My mother would begin cooking the Friday evening
meal early in the day. Whether the traditional meal of soup,
chicken, and potato pudding was served, or other dishes like
brisket of beef, veal roast, or fish with dill sauce, even the food
had to be special for the Sabbath. The Friday afternoon routine
had become standardized in our home. My mother would finish her
cooking while the children went upstairs to put on special clothes
to greet the Sabbath. My father would come home just in time to
leave for the synagogue with his sons. While the men of the house
attended evening services, the women set the table, lit the Sabbath
candles, and completed preparations for the Sabbath evening meal.

When we arrived home from the synagogue, my father would
walk in the door and sing out, 'Good Shabbos!' He would go around
the room and kiss each of the women and we would then sit around
the living room and talk briefly about whom we had seen at services.
Someone, usually my mother or father, would begin the singing of

OPPOSITE The blessing

ABOVE Learning how to make *challah*

ABOVE RIGHT The prayer for Shabbat

'*Shalom Aleichem*', a song praising the peace of the Sabbath. After the singing, my parents would bless each of the children in turn. I knew that the words of the blessing were pleas that God would see each of us through but I felt that the purpose of the blessings was to indicate that even though we might have had a good week or a bad one, they still loved us. The blessings were always followed by a kiss, one on the forehead from my mother, and three from my father, one on the forehead and one on each cheek.

Then the evening meal was served. It was always referred to as 'dinner', not 'supper' as it was called during the week. This added to the formality of the Sabbath observance and separated it from the rest of the week. My father recited the *kiddush*, the blessing over the wine, and passed cups of wine around, first to my mother, and after that in order of age – grandmothers, relatives, guests, and, finally, to the children. Then followed the ritual washing of the hands. After the blessing over the two loaves of *hallah* (always egg bread in our house) my father would cut the bread into at least five more pieces than there were people. If someone should drop by unexpectedly, there would be bread for him or her to eat. Curiously, the bread was doused with salt. I remember that as the bread plate was passed around the table, and everyone took a piece, we would have to shake it over the tablecloth to remove as much of the salt as possible. Until the bread had been tasted, no one was to speak and destroy the sanctity of the blessings. However, I usually spoke too soon and glares would come my way from all directions.

During the course of the meal, the conversations were many. I am left with the memory of gossiping about friends, neighbours, and relatives more than any distinct recollections of conversations. Towards the end of the meal, we would occasionally sing Sabbath *zemirot* (happy songs) in celebration of the holy day. Although celebrated weekly, we learned that the Sabbath was second in importance only to Yom Kippur (the Day of Atonement). The grace after meals followed the *zemirot* and was normally chanted after a brief discussion about which of the children should lead the family in this service. Usually, no one volunteered. Unlike our parents, we children had not experienced the Depression of the 1930s, and since our parents were economically secure, we had never known the atmosphere of a home without enough food. Having never known want, we could not quite see the need for a prayer to God thanking Him for our food. I now know how lucky we were, but at the time, the warmth and protection of my family shielded me from experiencing some of the harsher realities of the world.

Friday night was always family night in our home. We never went our separate ways after dinner but stayed together, sometimes merely to talk about the previous week's activities or those of the week ahead. Often we would play group participation games involving the entire family. On most occasions we would play verbal word games since writing is forbidden in the Orthodox household on the Sabbath; or sometimes card games, but always without gambling.

Costumes and customs are different, but Shabbat unites this Yemenite family in the same way as it unites the US family in the picture opposite

When we went to bed, we'd have to undress in the darkened room as the only available light source was one small overhead lamp in the hall that remained on throughout the Sabbath. I shared a room with my three brothers and most nights we played around in the bedroom after it was time to go to sleep. But on Friday nights, my parents didn't seem to mind our frivolity. After a very tiring evening, we drifted off to sleep. The routine of these evenings created an atmosphere of peace to which I can still return for comfort.

Saturday morning was also very special. We would wake and dress for morning services. Unlike Friday night, the women of the house also attended the Sabbath morning services. We would leave our house early, and begin the walk to the synagogue. Our first stop would always be at my grandmother's apartment a few blocks away. Along the way we would often meet others walking to synagogue, including the rabbi and his family. Once we reached the synagogue, my brothers and I prayed in the basement chapel, in our own Junior Congregation.

The Junior Congregation provided us with a real sense of community with our friends. Though the services were supervised by the educational director of the synagogue, we took an active part in the service. An older member of the congregation would come down to the chapel to chant the Torah portion in Hebrew for us, but the services were conducted completely by us. The rabbi

OPPOSITE A father teaching his seven children at home

Lighting the Shabbat candles on a kibbutz

always took some time to teach the weekly Torah portion. Though the Junior Congregation was not created to promote a sense of family togetherness, praying with my brothers made the service even more meaningful for me. Along with praying, we had a good time together talking and telling jokes.

After services, we would attend the *kiddush*, which was not just the blessing over the wine, but a feast of cookies and cakes. As the congregation gathered together again, I felt a sense of belonging to a larger Jewish community, something like a huge family. From the synagogue, we would either go home or to my grandmother's apartment for 'dinner', the Sabbath afternoon meal. After the meal, the activities varied. We would stay home and play or, more often, go visiting in the neighbourhood.

The Havdalah service that marks the end of the Sabbath and the resumption of the regular weekdays was the most moving spiritual experience of the Sabbath. There was not joy that the Sabbath was over, but a realization that the peace of the Sabbath was short and fleeting. The Sabbath was a time for relaxation, but the Sabbath had the added attractions of the enjoyment of services and the family togetherness that has always been a concrete part of my contentment. It is my hope that as a husband and father I will be able to share the same togetherness of the Sabbath that I had in my parents' home.

The Sabbath family consisted of the immediate family only: my parents, brothers and sister, and my grandmothers. But the major Jewish festivals, especially Passover, Sukkot, and Shavuot,

All sorts of boxes are pressed into service to make the *sukkah*

gained a special significance by gathering the relatives from out of town to our home to celebrate with us.

Before Sukkot we had great fun decorating our Sukkah, the traditional outdoor booth. It signifies, with its hanging fruits and vegetables, the tents constructed by the Jews in the wilderness during the forty-year march from Egypt to Israel, as well as the harvest season during which the celebration takes place.

This family cohesion held true for the other festivals and made the Passover *sedarim* one of my favourite experiences. We never had a *seder* with less than twenty people and although most of those at the meal were family members from all over the country, there were always a number of guests. Everyone took an active role in the *seder* service. My father led the service, but during the course of the *seder* we would read from the Haggadah in sequence, around the table. The Passover meal never varied from what my family has served for many generations: a hard-boiled egg doused with salt water, followed by gefilte fish with horse radish, chicken soup with matzo balls, a main course of turkey with stuffing, asparagus, and various sponge cakes for dessert. This meal could never be duplicated during the year with the same meaning. On more than one occasion I have taken a hard-boiled egg and doused it with salt water, but it has never tasted quite as good out of the context of the Passover *seder*.

The end of the *seder* service consists of a number of songs related to the holiday. Four full cups of wine were drunk during our *sedarim* so towards the end of the service when the singing began, a lack of sobriety added to the tumult. It was always a joy to hear a crowd of Jewish people celebrating their freedom, singing of their yearning to be reunited in Israel. Though Passover recalls a time when the Jews endured much suffering, it also proclaims our liberation.

Pouring towards the Western Wall for Shavuot, one of the Pilgrim Festivals when a trip to Jerusalem should be undertaken if possible

The third major festival, Shavuot, was significant in my memory largely in terms of the delicious meals that my mother and grandmothers would prepare. The evening meals would always consist of dairy dishes: fried fish, blintzes, noodle pudding, and farmer's salad. But the biggest meal of the festival was the 'dinner' served in the afternoon: roast duckling. This meal was served only once a year and we all looked forward to it with excitement.

It may seem from my memory as if all of Judaism centres around eating. This, of course, is not true. The family, in Judaic tradition, is the focal point of individual activity. It is with his or her family that the individual receives his or her earliest training: reverence for life, respect for fellow men, and knowledge of the Jewish heritage. In the Jewish home there is a constant effort to impress upon children the meaning of Judaism in everyday life, the adherence to the commandments of the Torah, the reliance upon the guardian of the Jewish people, their God, and the need for prayer to better one's self and one's relationship not only to God but to the people with whom one has contact in everyday life situations. It is in school that one learns facts and figures and dates and places, but it is from the family that one learns love and wisdom. It is a tribute to Judaism and the Jewish family that it makes the simple act of eating into an occasion for a real sense of shared emotion and a renewed reverence for God.

Just before my *bar mitzvah*, however, I began to question just about everything in my life including my family and Judaism. I would ask questions of my family about being a Jew, hoping that they could explain why we were different. I recall asking, 'Why must I stay home on Friday night while Neil and Jimmy and Robbie are going to Frisch's Restaurant for dinner and then sleeping over at Richie's house?' The answer to that question, and others like it, was always the same, 'Because that is the way that we practice our lives as Jews!' Looking back, I see that my family had consciously set aside the Sabbath as a time during each week that the family could share in peace. When I was twelve, however, I only saw that others were enjoying things that were forbidden to me.

As I approached thirteen, the questions that I asked myself and my family became even broader. The entire question of prescribed religion where someone, somewhere, sometime, set down a series of rules that through a series of births I was obligated to follow annoyed me. It troubled me, as it often still does, to be born into a religion, into a country, into a community, into a congregation, into a family, all of which seemed to restrict my individuality, my freedom to be myself.

All these questions remained unresolved when I began the formal preparation for my *bar mitzvah* in the summer of 1961. I attended a course offered at the religious school during the summer mornings for all of us who would be *bar* and *bat mitzvah* the next year. Our teacher began the first class by saying that the synagogue would be

OPPOSITE Passover *seder* in a Bukharan family

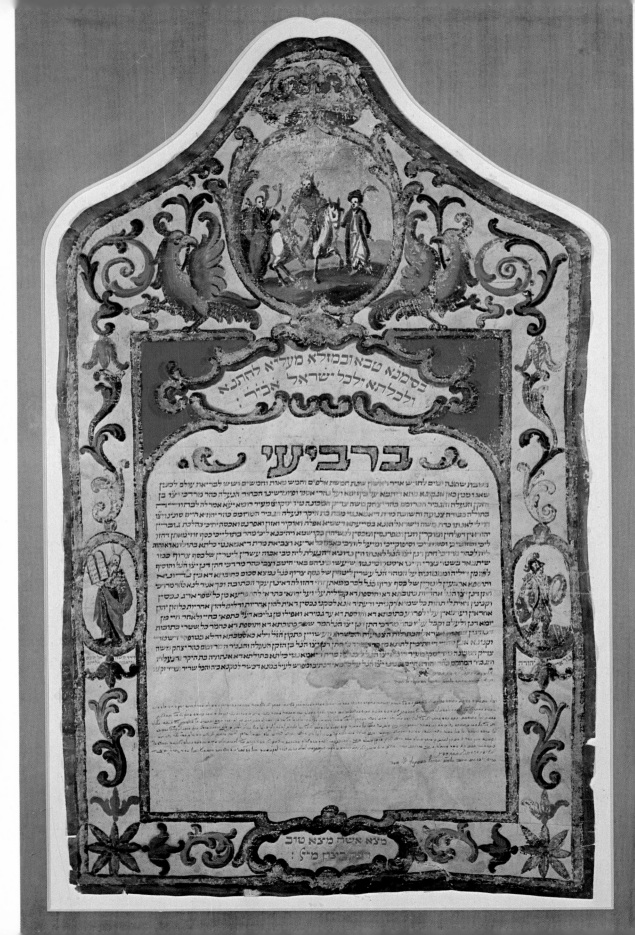

בסימנא טבא ובמזלא מעליא
בסימנא טבא ילכל ישראל להתגא
ולכלתא ילכל ישראל אביר :

ברביעי

בעשבת שמנה ימים לחודש אדר ואשית שנת חמשת אלפים וחמש מאות וחמשים ושש לבריאת עולם לכינן
שאנו מנין כאן אקטא מתא דיתפא על פי ימא ועל אדרי ימא ופריומיט הבחור הנעלה מהר מרדכי ילד בן
הזקן והנעלה והגביר המרומם כהרי יצחק משה צדיק הנבהם טד יקרי שמעיר רומא יפא אמר לה לברתהוו --- דה
בתורה כבירה צנועה וחשובה מד ח דאשמאנוזי מבת כת ליקר ונעלה והגביר המרומם כהר יהו אהיים סינינרוט
יהי לי לאנתו כדת משה וישראל ואנא נדונא בסייעתיה דשמיא אפלח ואוקיר ואזון ואפרנם ואכסה יתיכי נדלכת גוברין
יהודאין דפלחין ומוקרין וזנין ומפרנסין ומכסין לנשיהון בקושטא ויהיבנא ליכי מהר בתוליכי כסף זווי מאתן דחזו
ליכי מדחואי וכ ופסותיכי ומיקייכי וסיפוקיכי ומיעל לותיכי כאשפ כל ארעא ודבריח מרית דאנאנגי כלתא בתולת נאדאותה
ליתו לבהר מרדבי חתן י רק יצו הבל לאבהתו הין נדונא דהנעלת ליה מבי אתה עשרין ליטרין של כסף צרוף כמור
שיתמאר משטי גברי ה יכו איסטו ן טיב גמד שי אעשו בבהם באר חיסט וצבי מהר מרדכי חתן דנן יצו הבל והוסיף
לה מן י ילי דילמה ומת נותוניה על ה המותי הבל עשירין ליטשין של כסף צרוק נם טא סבום כתובדא דא בויק נד -- וכא
ורה בהמתא אר מעץ ליטרין של כסף צרוק הבל לבר ממאתן דעי דהדזו להד איטא עקר הכתובה וכך אמר לנא מהר י כך
מיתן דינק צה הרי ו הבל אחריות כתובהא דא וחוספתא ו הקבלית עלי וער ל הרי יהוא בתר א לה פרי מן כל שפר ארג נבסין
וקנטיג ו אית לי תהות כל שמיא דקנייתי וד עתיר א ובא לק מקנ נכסין דאית להון אחריותן ודלית להון אחריותן יהו
אחראין ערב נאם על ל כל למר עבכרסהא דא והוספתא דא ע גמירא ואפילו מן גלימא די על כתפאי כחיי ולאחר חיי מן
יומא דנן ולע ולם וקבל עלי ו כהו מרדכי חתן וכן יצו הבל והמד שצר פרטריתא דא ותוסטת דא כחומר כל שטרי כתובות
המ מהדגן ואער א דכפבהדלות הצבא הלח הטשראות ו עשויין ן תקנין הזל ו ילא כאסמכתא ה דלא כטופטי דישטרי
וקנגנא את מ כהו חד י ח יהודכיו לתהבא מן מאדכ יא ד חתן דנן וצו הבל ד בן הזקן הנעלה והגביר ה הר ומבו מהר יצחק משה
צדיק הנבהם ל וד סוכ יפ מעיר רומא ל מבר דני י הבל ל ע הבל מרה י אבא וגי דכי לתא כתור התא דא אהתרותזהו כתהיקר ר נעלה
הגב ד המחותם כלי תורה חיד ביבם וער חיבם ובתכבובהם לעיל במה דכשר למקנא ביה והבל שריר וקיים

מצא אשה מצא טוב
מאתו יונתן מיל

'our home away from home' and that it is the Jew's life duty to always maintain strong ties to the synagogue. But in my questioning, I was already rebelling against my home so the rabbi's words had an ironic twist, asking me to rebel against the synagogue as well.

The *bar mitzvah* preparation course dwelt on the responsibilities and duties of becoming a Jewish adult. Not that we were expected to undertake all these responsibilities at once, but to get a taste of what would be expected of us as adults and to learn that we were *responsible* for our own actions. These demands seemed out of line with what we were asked to do in the secular world where our only responsibilities were to swim away the hot summer afternoons. I was perplexed by the gap between what was expected of me and what was expected of my friends, and by the distance between what the secular world and what my religion demanded. My *bar mitzvah* passed in this confused period of my life without meaning a great deal to me beyond being another happy occasion, drawing the family together in celebration.

It wasn't until almost a year later that the meaning of *bar mitzvah* took on more weight in my mind. When I learned that the father of one of my friends had died, I felt an urgent need to be with my friend as soon as possible, but I also felt frightened. I left religious school with several friends on the afternoon we heard the news and walked the mile or so to our friend's house for the evening services. As we walked, we talked about everything we could think of except the purpose of our walk. Once we got within a few blocks of the house, the reality of the situation took hold. What were we to do and what were we to say? Should we go at all? Fortunately, we had some extra time on our hands so we stopped into a pizza parlour a block from the house. Four young, inexperienced kids had to make a rather important decision and we needed time to think about it. We had no idea what our friend was going through as none of us had lost a parent.

After a sombre discussion, we decided on our course of action. We went to the services, each kissed our friend, and said nothing. The services began after some small talk among the many people attending the first service after the funeral. The rabbi led the services in a dignified manner, pausing now and again to make personal and kind remarks about the deceased. Since this man had died quite unexpectedly at a relatively young age, the shock and emotional tension were greater than if he had been ill for a long period or a man in his eighties.

Near the end of the service, the rabbi asked our friend to rise and say the mourner's *kaddish*, the prayer for the dead that mentions nothing about death. My friend rose and recited the prayer in a frightened, uncertain, trembling voice I will never forget. The rabbi then turned to the recently *bar mitzvah* young man and told him that he would now be responsible for his family, that he was now 'the man of the house'. Part of me trembled as I wondered if I

ABOVE Traditional wedding rings

OPPOSITE The heart of the family, the bridal couple

could take on the responsibility if I lost my own father. But part of me also thought of how the young man's family, the congregation, and the whole community were already rallying around him and giving him the support he would need. Somehow, I felt I understood a little more what it meant to be a 'mensch', a Jewish man. All the history, customs, duties, and responsibilities that had been weighing so heavily on me were now helping my friend through his crisis and I knew that they would help me through mine.

I am now twenty-five and I have much to be grateful for. I look back at my past and think about those factors that had the greatest influence on me. I need look no farther than my family. They guided me in my everyday activities, and by watching and scrutinizing and listening to them, I learned a concern for my fellow man, a reverence for their religious convictions, and, most important, a love of life.

The close relationship with my family has been associated with joy, tribulation, sorrow, contentment, confusion, and rebellion. Despite, or because of, all these emotions, my primary feeling is gratification. It is through their love and guidance that I want to emulate their lives in my own. I want to show my gratitude to them by raising a family of my own and to do for my children what my family did for me: teach them that love of life is love of God, and that love of God is love of Judaism, and that love of Judaism is love of life.

LOUIS J. PEERLESS

Some Yiddish Proverbs

A job is fine, but it interferes with your time.

Your health comes first – you can always hang yourself later.

Sleep faster, we need the pillows.

Truth rests with God alone, and a little with me.

If God were living on earth, people would break His windows.

If the ass had horns and the ox knew his strength, the world would be done for.

A man should live, if only to satisfy his curiosity.

If you can't bite, don't show your teeth.

God never told anyone to be stupid.

Shrouds are made without pockets.

translated by ISADORE GOLDSTICK

The Mystic Way

Because of its stress on the Law, particularly on those aspects which cover the details of daily life, Judaism has sometimes been scornfully called 'pot-and-pan-theism'. Yet there is another aspect of Judaism, which also has an all-embracing effect on Jewish life. This is mysticism, the Kabbalah. It has always been understood, however, that the mystic way could be a dangerous one. The longing for the Messiah could too easily lead men to hail him in the person of a charismatic leader. After the false claim of Shabbetai Zevi in the seventeenth century, some rabbis feared that mysticism was the road to error, although in the eighteenth century the tradition was revitalized in the Hasidic movement. This too caused divisions among Jews. When Jewish history was first properly studied, in the nineteenth century, it was a time when mysticism was avoided as irrational. Nowadays, when there is renewed interest in mystical approaches, especially among young people, it is time for Jews to confront once more their own mystical tradition.

'Sometimes a man in a very deep sleep can be awakened only by the secrets of the Torah'

RABBI NAHMAN OF BRATSLAV

The Barrier of Senses

Looking at the physical world, we see mountains and lakes, great deserts and immense oceans, and in the interior of the Earth is fire. Looking upwards, we see the sun, the moon and the other planets of the solar system. Beyond are the stars which compose our galaxy; and further beyond are other galaxies.

This is what we are able to perceive with the Five Senses we possess; yet this is not the only reality. If we had other senses, senses we cannot imagine – for they are totally outside our experience – we would see the universe in a totally different way. For instance – picture what the world might look like to a creature with an eye sensitive only to radio waves. Further, even with the five senses we have, if we interpret their messages to the mind in a different way, we see a different world. This is what happens when someone experiences an hallucination, or a vision.

The One Reality

It therefore seems that there is not just one way of seeing – there are countless different ways of seeing. But always what we are looking at is the One Reality – though it clothes itself in different forms. The One is infinite: even in the way we normally see our universe we can find no limit. The One is formless – yet it clothes itself in all the forms we see. It is infinite power; it is pure Being. For this reason the Hebrew name of God is a form of the verb 'to be'.

OPPOSITE Ezekiel's vision (see p. 72)

It all depends on how you look. This picture, known as the Winson Figure, might depict a face in profile or a standing figure

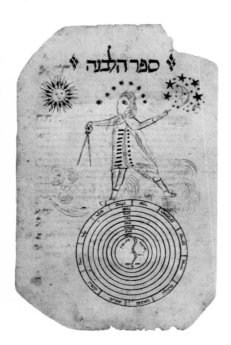

ABOVE The frontispiece of an astrological manuscript

OPPOSITE Mystics visualized the worlds without number as spreading out in concentric circles from the Infinite, *Ein Sof*

The One in its infinite formlessness cannot be expressed in words: words can only describe something which has some form, some attribute. But the way in which it clothes itself can be described to some extent. We can describe the world that we see in our ordinary lives – this too is a manifestation of the One. And certain men, learned in Torah, have been able to describe other worlds, visionary worlds, in which the infinite power and the hidden nature of the One are revealed more openly. Such men are mystics.

In Jewish mysticism, the God is called *Ein Sof*, 'Without End', for the Infinite can have no beginning or end, no shape or form. Like a light which is so bright that to look directly at it would be blinding, God veils his radiance so that it becomes dimmer and bearable to the eyes. This veiling takes place in four stages, called worlds – for at each stage a different world is created. There are four worlds, just as there are four letters in the Hebrew name of God.

In each of the Four Worlds there are ten aspects which reveal the different attributes of the power of the Infinite as it is expressed within that World. They are like coloured veils in front of a source of white light. Through each veil a different colour is seen; yet the light itself is not coloured – for the Infinite has no attributes.

At the lowest aspect of the lowest World, the light of the *Ein Sof* is at its most dim. This lowest aspect, this lowest manifestation of the Infinite, is our limitless cosmos. In the cosmos are countless galaxies; in each galaxy are myriads of stars; and we live on a single planet in such a galaxy. Yet man, a mere speck at the end of a mighty chain of being, himself contains the very essence of the Infinite. Thus the lowest is the same as the highest, and all is Unity.

Nowadays, science has taught us that we can travel through more of the immense space that surrounds us than was ever before thought possible. Through science-fiction stories we are able to imagine too that it might be possible to travel through time. Therefore, we are beginning to understand that the ordinary world we see with our eyes is not all we can learn to know, that keeping our feet firmly on the ground is not always the best way to understanding.

Centuries ago, the sages of the Torah knew that there was a way to approach infinity. So that people could grasp what they meant, they expressed their perceptions through stories, and poetic visions.

Visions:Ezekiel

Surrounded by the Infinite, and filled by the Infinite, man sleeps; like a child asleep in a darkened room, for the Infinite is veiled. But when the curtain or Veil is drawn back and bright light fills the room, the sleeper awakes. What he sees might be called a vision: it is, in effect, a higher manifestation of the Infinite.

Thus Ezekiel, in exile after the destruction of the First Temple, saw a manifestation of one of the four visionary worlds. Here is a free translation from the first chapter of his book:

On the fifth of Tammuz, while I was by the River Kvar, the heavens opened and I saw visions of God. From the North there came a great storm cloud, flickering with fire; the edge of the cloud was bright like the colour of lightning, and surrounding the whole cloud were shining bands of colour, blue, green, yellow and red, like a rainbow. Inside the cloud were the shapes of four beings made of flames bright as lightning, surrounded by rainbow colours. The beings seemed to flicker forward and backward, approaching and retreating, like lightning. Each being had the body of a man, but its head had four different faces: in front was the face of a man, to the right the face of a lion, to the left the face of an ox; and the back of their heads had the face of an eagle. They each had four wings, with human hands underneath the wings; and instead of ordinary legs each of the beings had just one straight leg, ending in a hoof like the hoof of a calf.

Beneath each of the beings was a shining wheel, which was also alive, and all round the rims of the wheels were eyes like human eyes, which could see. Each of the beings controlled the wheel which was underneath it.

A kind of canopy, or platform, was spread out over the heads of the four beings. The canopy looked as if it were made of cold, terrifying ice. I could hear the sound of the wings of the beings under the canopy, and it was like the sound of a great waterfall, or of an immense crowd of people.

Above the canopy there was a shining blue throne, which looked as if it were made of sapphire. And on the throne was the form of a man, the colour of lightning, surrounded by rainbow colours.

All this was within the cloud. It was a vision of the Glory of God, and I saw, and I fell on my face in fear; and then I heard a Voice speaking . . .

Down through the ages, men have been impressed by Ezekiel's account of his stupendous vision. But they have found it hard to understand, and those who were unable to accept that the prophet saw the glory of God have tried to offer rational explanations for it. One man has even suggested recently that Ezekiel saw the landing of space travellers from another world! In a sense he is right. It *was* another world which Ezekiel saw, one normally hidden from men, but one which the mystic can perceive.

The Neshamah (Soul)

The power revealed by such a manifestation makes man afraid, for it is human nature to be afraid of what you cannot understand. If man continues to think of himself as a separate entity, unconnected with the One, he will find such a revelation harmful, for nothing can stand against that power.

But the One is within man: in his *Neshamah*, a word which literally means breath: man has within him his soul, the breath of the deepest essence of the Infinite. Just as the light of the *Ein Sof* is hidden from the material world, so too a veil hides the light of the

Neshamah from its outer manifestations, man's mind and physical body. This veil is the ego, the Self.

The ego thus forms a barrier between the visionary worlds of the *Neshamah* and those of the *Ein Sof*. It also separates the consciousness of man from the hidden aspects in his soul. The Hebrew word for the ego, I, is *Aniy*. The word for Nothing is *Ayin*, which is composed of the same three Hebrew letters. *Aniy* can be changed into *Ayin*; the ego can be annihilated, made nothing. This giving up of the power of the ego is expressed by the prostration of the prophet before God. For if the ego stands in the way of the immense power of the Infinite, a man cannot reach fulfilment.

Man does not have to remain physically prostrate; he is able to get up and move, but now it is not the ego which directs his behaviour. He is no longer a servant of his ego; he is a servant of God.

We have seen that between the visionary worlds of the *Neshamah* and those of the *Ein Sof* there is a barrier: the ordinary physical world; that is, ordinary consciousness of the physical world.

The Dead Sea, home of one of the earliest Jewish mystic groups. They were known as 'Riders in the Chariot' because they meditated on the image of the chariot that carried Elijah to heaven and struggled to follow his path by visionary means

When this barrier is an ordinary one it blocks the path of the power of the *Ein Sof* and the *Neshamah*. But when it ceases to be ordinary, when it becomes sacred – then it is no longer a barrier. Torah ritual makes the physical world sacred, for through ritual it takes on the characteristics of the visionary worlds.

The Veil makes the world seem ordinary. The ego makes consciousness seem ordinary. The Hebrew word *kadosh* means non-ordinary, special, sacred. Through ritual the consciousness of the world becomes *kadosh*. It is then no longer a barrier, and man is in unity with the Infinite.

The Torah

Rabbi Akiva, who alone entered Pardes in peace and alone came out in peace

Moses came closer than any man to the Infinite. In unity with the Infinite, and with the Infinite acting through him, he wrote the Torah. The Torah teaches us the way to join oneself to God.

The Torah is itself spoken of as a universe: a sacred universe, revealed through letters and words, stories and Commandments. In the Torah, the Veil hiding the light of the Infinite is absent: for the Torah is wholly sacred, and there is nothing ordinary in it.

Therefore when a man sets aside his ego (his own veil) and unites with the Torah, he is in union with all the worlds – both those within him and those beyond.

When a man carries out a ritual Commandment, the light of the Infinite passes through him. This light is felt as joy, *Simchah*. The joy we feel in learning and keeping the Torah is the joy of the *Ein Sof* itself.

There is a right and a wrong way to do everything. The dangers of entering the secrets of Torah in the wrong way are illustrated in a story told in the Talmud:

Four men entered Pardes, the realm of the highest secrets of the Torah: Ben Azai, Ben Zoma, Acher (Elisha ben Abuyah) and Rabbi Akiva. Ben Azai looked and died; Ben Zoma looked and went mad; Acher became an atheist. But Rabbi Akiva alone entered in peace and came out in peace.

Rabbi Simeon bar Yochai was a disciple of Rabbi Akiva. For twelve years he and his son hid in a cave, contemplating secret worlds. During this period he wrote the Zohar, the greatest of Jewish mystical books. When they emerged from the cave, they saw people ploughing the fields and Rabbi Simeon said: 'They busy themselves with the transient world, and forget the eternal world!' Whatever they looked at burst into flames. A voice from Heaven said: 'Have you come out to destroy My World? Return to your cave!' They went back for another year. When they finally came out they saw people keeping the Torah, which unifies the worlds, and gives even the transient world the illumination of eternity: then their minds found peace.

Good and Evil

A Midrash tells that when God created the world, He said: If I create the world with the attribute of Mercy only, then evil will increase (for there will be no punishment); if I create it with the attribute of Severity only, how will it be able to survive? So I will create it with both attributes.

The Zohar tells us that the Torah is a kind of 'blueprint' for the whole of Creation. The 613 Commandments in the Torah are like 613 strands of a cord which connect the world to God. By keeping each Commandment light and life-force flow, from the infinite radiance of God, into the world.

Just as Creation consists of the two attributes of Mercy (revealing light) and Severity (concealment), so we find two kinds of Commandment: Positive (things one *should* do), corresponding to Mercy; and Negative (things one should *not* do), corresponding to Severity.

Through keeping the Commandments a person is wrapping himself in the radiance of God, and directly connecting with the essence of the Infinite.

The distinction between Mercy and Severity is the source of the distinction between happiness and suffering. But the mystic sees beyond this distinction; he sees that in truth all is One. Whatever happens to him he considers as good: for he knows that everything is from the One Source – God. This is a change of *perception*: other people perceive a distinction between good and bad events, but the Jewish mystic sees only that the light of the Infinite fills them both. Rabbi Nahman of Bratslav said that such a man (as long as he is not fooling himself) is living even now, in this World, in the time of the Messiah and the World to Come. Thus this World and the World to come are unified: this is the goal of Judaism.

There is a Hasidic story of a man who could not understand why the Talmud says that when something bad happens one should

The tomb of Simeon bar Yochai at Meron, Galilee

75

bless God. He was told to ask Rabbi Zusya of Hannipol, a Hasidic teacher who was known by everyone to have suffered very much in his life from extreme poverty and need. The man found Rabbi Zusya and asked his question. Rabbi Zusya answered: 'How can I know the answer to that? Thank God I have enjoyed only happiness throughout my life. I advise you to go and ask someone who has experienced suffering.'

Such a man too was Nahum of Gamzu, the teacher of Rabbi Akiva. Whatever happened to him he would say, 'This too is for good!' (*Gam zu le-tovah*).

Mercy is the particular attribute of Abraham and Severity is that of Isaac.

Jacob, whose other name, Israel, is that of the whole Jewish people, unites both these attributes. The path of Jewish mysticism is the path of Jacob.

The Kelippot

The manifestations of the Infinite that we have spoken about so far are all holy: they lead man closer to the One. But there are also other, unholy, manifestations – which lead man away from the One. They are the source of spiritual evil and give rise to evil visions.

These unholy manifestations are called the *Kelippot*, a Hebrew word meaning 'shells' or 'husks'. They are the backward, negative aspects which the Infinite manifests. Their source too, like everything in all the worlds, is the pure light of the Infinite within them.

The *Kelippot* are sometimes called guardians of the holy aspects of the Infinite – just as a shell guards the nut within, the Jew, through Torah and the Commandments, breaks through the power of the *Kelippot* and raises them to the Holiness. The mystic must be able to break through their power.

Acher, who after entering Pardes became an atheist, failed in this task. He had been caught by the *Kelippot* and was unable to escape.

When the Temple was destroyed and the Jews went into exile, the Presence of God which dwelt in the Temple, the *Shekhinah*, went into exile with them. Like her people, she languishes among the harsh *Kelippot*, yearning to return to the Holy One, just as the Jews yearn for Redemption. The separation of the *Shekhinah* from the Holy One and her yearning for release from exile are described in Song of Songs, which Rabbi Akiva called the holiest of all the holy books. In this passage from Chapter 5, the *Shekhinah* is speaking. The 'guardians' are the *Kelippot*.

I was asleep, but my heart was awake. Suddenly I heard the voice of my lover, tapping softly on the door, saying 'Open for me, my beautiful one; my hair is wet with dew of the night'. I got up to open for him; my fingers dripped myrrh on the bolt. But when I opened the door he had slipped away into the darkness. My soul yearned for him; I went out to look for him

but could not find him, I called his name but he did not answer. The guardians patrolling the city found me wandering; they hit me and beat me and stripped off my clothes. Daughters of Jerusalem, promise me that if you find my lover you will tell him I am sick with love for him . . .

A Hasidic bride. The bride is a very important mystic image. The Sabbath comes as the bride of Israel and the *Shekhinah* too is sometimes seen as the bride who followed the Jewish people into exile

Some Mystics

Four hundred years ago Safed in Galilee was the centre of Jewish mysticism, known as the Kabbalah, 'the tradition'. Mystics are called kabbalists. Like all other aspects of Judaism, mysticism involves study. Mystics did not go off alone to wait for the light of the Infinite to strike them. They knew that they travelled on a hard road, that illumination would not come if they just sat around and waited for it. Therefore they banded together, studying the teachings of previous sages, using all the intellectual powers that God had given them in their efforts to unravel His mysteries.

In Safed lived the most important kabbalists of the time: Rabbi Moses Cordovero, his disciple Rabbi Joseph Caro (author of the *Shulchan Arukh*, the code of Jewish Law; see p. 49) and above all, Rabbi Isaac Luria. He was the greatest kabbalist since Rabbi Simeon bar Yochai, and delved into the cause of the manifestation of all the worlds which veil the light of the *Ein Sof*. He also entered into the secrets of the nature of the *Kelippot*, which he perceived as remnants of destroyed worlds, kept in existence by the Light of *Ein Sof* trapped among them. The task of man is to raise this Light back to its source in the Infinite, and then the *Kelippot* cease to exist. Some *Kelippot* are too strong to be destroyed now: they will be annihilated only at the End of Days. Like Jewish mystics before (and after) him, but in his own particular way, Rabbi Isaac Luria also taught the kabbalistic meanings in every detail of Jewish Law. By following the Law in all its meanings, man can set free the light trapped in the *Kelippot*. That is, he can fulfil the task for which man was created.

Two hundred years ago Rabbi Israel Baal Shem, called the Baal Shem Tov, lived in the Ukraine. He wandered from village to

OPPOSITE The wedding dance from the film *Fiddler on the Roof*

RIGHT Hasidim dance for joy outside the shrine Simeon bar Yochai

BELOW Students and hippies join in the dancing of the Lubavitcher Hasidim in Brooklyn, New York, to see if they too can taste that holy joy

village teaching a path of mysticism higher than all other paths, for he showed how a man can cut straight through every barrier and reach the *Ein Sof* Itself. His followers are called Hasidim ('pious ones').

The Baal Shem Tov told a story of a king who had surrounded himself with the appearance of high walls; they were only optical illusions, but people thought they were real, and tried in vain to find the entrance to the fortress. But then there came a man who saw the truth, that the walls of the fortress were not real. He did not look for the entrance, but walked straight through to the king.

God hides Himself behind many obstacles; but they have no reality, and any man can pierce straight through them and be at once in the very presence of God.

The great grandson of the Baal Shem Tov was Rabbi Nahman of Bratslav. In one of his teachings he says that although a man struggles to perceive the light of the *Ein Sof,* his mind, which cannot bear this light, tries to prevent him. But through the immense joy that comes from keeping the Commandments, he is able to annihilate part of his mind, forming nine great empty halls in it, into which the light of the *Ein Sof* can enter. Only non-mind, the void, can grasp the *Ein Sof.* He said: 'The goal of knowledge is *not to know.*'

The Baal Shem Tov's main disciple was Rabbi Dov Baer, the Great Maggid of Mezritch. He said that the ordinary kabbalist is like a man with many keys, with which he tries to open the doors of the hidden worlds. But the Hasid is like a man with an axe, who breaks down all barriers in order to reach the highest Unity. Then, said Rabbi Dov Baer, that man is above Time, and above Life and Death.

The Infinite is within man's own soul. If he only can see this, then the veils within him which hide it are swept away, and the infinite Light is revealed.

God is hiding in everything, even in the worst and lowest thing. But if man knows that He is hiding there – then He is no longer hidden.

The light of the *Ein Sof* is hidden even in the deepest of the *Kelippot.* Thus even sin, the most terrible *Kelippah*, conceals within it the light of Repentance. When a person discovers this, and repents with his whole heart, then he has reached the secret of the World to Come in this world.

The chief disciple of the Great Maggid was Rabbi Schneur Zalman of Lyady, the founder of the Habad (Lubavitch) path of Hasidism.

Once Rabbi Schneur Zalman found one of his disciples weeping. When asked what was wrong, the disciple replied that he could not understand a certain difficult passage in his master's mystical teaching. Rabbi Schneur Zalman then sang him a Hasidic song (*niggun*) which was the essence of that teaching; then the disciple was able to understand.

OPPOSITE A Jew at prayer, painted by Marc Chagall, whose paintings reflect much of the Hasidic vision

OPPOSITE Hasidim in Jerusalem.

It is the nature of the world that men are not totally alone, but are able to help and lead each other along the paths which lead to the Infinite. The followers of a Hasidic Rebbe (or *zaddik*) gains spiritual power from him, just as a flame gains power from a brighter flame. Each Rebbe shows a different path; but like the many different worlds, all these paths express the One Unity.

Rabbi Schneur Zalman's present-day descendant is the Lubavitcher Rebbe, who lives in New York. He has written many books showing the relevance of Jewish mysticism today. Apart from his great knowledge of mysticism he also studied science at university. Thousands of Hasidim all over the world transmit these teachings to the people. A unique aspect of Lubavitch is that many Lubavitch Hasidim come from non-orthodox backgrounds. Through mysticism – usually called *Hassidus* – a modern Jew is able to see the relevance and meaning in his religion.

On the one hand, Hasidic mysticism is an intense yearning for union with God. Rabbi Schneur Zalman would be visibly overcome by ecstatic states of spiritual longing during which he would exclaim 'I do not want anything else! I want neither This World nor The World to Come, I desire nothing but You alone!' Yet of the very same man another story is told which illustrated how much Hasidism is part of this world:

His son and successor, Rabbi Dovber of Lubavitch, lived with him for many years. Rabbi Dovber was once so deeply engrossed in his meditations and learning that he did not hear the weeping of a child that had fallen from its cradle in the very same room. Rabbi Schneur Zalman was upstairs at the time, also deeply involved in his study. None the less he *did* hear the child. He went dow stairs, picked it up and put it back into its cradle. Then he said to his son: 'To be so engrossed in learning and meditation is indeed very lofty. Yet one should never lose oneself so much as not to hear the cries of a child'. This combination of yearning for God and yet being part of the world is the direction and goal of Jewish mysticism, the soul of Jewish life.

In order to teach the Hidden Torah, the Hasidim would tell stories. Here is one by Rabbi Nahman:

One day a king said to his chief minister: By astrology I see that whoever eats any of this year's harvest will go mad. So what shall we do? The chief minister suggested they should let everyone else eat the food, but they themselves should get food from another country. The king said: But if they are all mad, and only we two are not mad, it will be exactly as if we are mad and they are sane. So this is what we will do: the people will eat the food, and we will also eat it. But you and I will each put a sign on our foreheads, so that when we see the sign we will at least *know* that we are mad.

NAFTALI LOEWENTHAL

The Angel Levine

Manischevitz, a tailor, in his fifty-first year suffered many reverses and indignities. Previously a man of comfortable means, he overnight lost all he had, when his establishment caught fire and, after a metal container of cleaning fluid exploded, burned to the ground. Although Manischevitz was insured against fire, damage suits by two customers who had been hurt in the flames deprived him of every penny he had collected. At almost the same time, his son, of much promise, was killed in the war, and his daughter, without so much as a word of warning, married a lout and disappeared with him as off the face of the earth. Thereafter Manischevitz was victimized by excruciating backaches and found himself unable to work even as a presser – the only kind of work available to him – for more than an hour or two daily, because beyond that the pain from standing became maddening. His Fanny, a good wife and mother, who had taken in washing and sewing, began before his eyes to waste away. Suffering shortness of breath, she at last became seriously ill and took to her bed. The doctor, a former customer of Manischevitz, who out of pity treated them, at first had difficulty diagnosing her ailment but later put it down as hardening of the arteries at an advanced stage. He took Manischevitz aside, prescribed complete rest for her, and in whispers gave him to know there was little hope.

Throughout his trials Manischevitz had remained somewhat stoic, almost unbelieving that all this had descended upon his head, as if it were happening, let us say, to an acquaintance or some distant relative; it was in sheer quantity of woe incomprehensible. It was also ridiculous, unjust, and because he had always been a religious man, it was in a way an affront to God. Manischevitz believed this in all his suffering. When his burden had grown too crushingly heavy to be borne he prayed in his chair with shut hollow eyes: 'My dear God, sweetheart, did I deserve that this should happen to me?' Then recognizing the worthlessness of it,

The Lower East Side, New York,
Manischevitz's home, as it used to be

he put aside the complaint and prayed humbly for assistance: 'Give Fanny back her health, and to me for myself that I shouldn't feel pain in every step. Help now or tomorrow is too late. This I don't have to tell you.' And Manischevitz wept.

Manischevitz's flat, which he had moved into after the disastrous fire, was a meagre one, furnished with a few sticks of chairs, a table, and bed, in one of the poorer sections of the city. There were three rooms: a small, poorly-papered living room; an apology for a kitchen, with a wooden icebox; and the comparatively large bedroom where Fanny lay in a sagging secondhand bed, gasping for breath. The bedroom was the warmest room of the house and it was here, after his outburst to God, that Manischevitz, by the light of two small bulbs overhead, sat reading his Jewish newspaper. He was not truly reading, because his thoughts were everywhere; however the print offered a convenient resting place for his eyes, and a word or two, when he permitted himself to comprehend them, had the momentary effect of helping him forget his troubles. After a short while he discovered, to his surprise, that he was actively scanning the news, searching for an item of great interest to him. Exactly what he thought he would read he couldn't say – until he realized, with some astonishment, that he was expecting to discover something about himself. Manischevitz put his paper down and looked up with the distinct impression that someone had entered the apartment, though he could not remember having heard the sound of the door opening. He looked around: the room was very still, Fanny sleeping, for once, quietly. Half-frightened, he watched her until he was satisfied she wasn't dead; then, still disturbed by the thought of an unannounced visitor, he stumbled into the living

The Lower East Side today

room and there had the shock of his life, for at the table sat a Negro reading a newspaper he had folded up to fit into one hand.

'What do you want here?' Manischevitz asked in fright.

The Negro put down the paper and glanced up with a gentle expression. 'Good evening.' He seemed not to be sure of himself, as if he had got into the wrong house. He was a large man, bonily built, with a heavy head covered by a hard derby, which he made no attempt to remove. His eyes seemed sad, but his lips, above which he wore a slight moustache, sought to smile; he was not otherwise prepossessing. The cuffs of his sleeves, Manischevitz noted, were frayed to the lining and the dark suit was badly fitted. He had very large feet. Recovering from his fright, Manischevitz guessed he had left the door open and was being visited by a case worker from the Welfare Department – some came at night – for he had recently applied for relief. Therefore he lowered himself into a chair opposite the Negro, trying, before the man's uncertain smile, to feel comfortable. The former tailor sat stiffly but patiently at the table, waiting for the investigator to take out his pad and pencil and begin asking questions; but before long he became convinced the man intended to do nothing of the sort.

'Who are you?' Manischevitz at last asked uneasily.

'If I may, in so far as one is able to, identify myself, I bear the name of Alexander Levine.'

In spite of all his troubles Manischevitz felt a smile growing on his lips. 'You said Levine?' he politely inquired.

The Negro nodded. 'That is exactly right.'

Carrying the jest farther, Manischevitz asked, 'You are maybe Jewish?'

A bona fide angel of God, within prescribed limitations

'All my life I was, willingly.'

The tailor hesitated. He had heard of black Jews but had never met one. It gave an unusual sensation.

Recognizing in afterthought something odd about the tense of Levine's remark, he said doubtfully, 'You ain't Jewish anymore?'

Levine at this point removed his hat, revealing a very white part in his black hair, but quickly replaced it. He replied, 'I have recently been disincarnated into an angel. As such, I offer you my humble assistance, if to offer is within my province and ability – in the best sense.' He lowered his eyes in apology. 'Which calls for added explanation: I am what I am granted to be, and at present the completion is in the future.'

'What kind of angel is this?' Manischevitz gravely asked.

'A bona fide angel of God, within prescribed limitations,' answered Levine, 'not to be confused with the members of any particular sect, order, or organization here on earth operating under a similar name.'

Manischevitz was thoroughly disturbed. He had been expecting something but not this. What sort of mockery was it – provided Levine was an angel – of a faithful servant who had from childhood lived in the synagogues, always concerned with the word of God?

Fanny again lay supine, breathing with
blue-lipped difficulty

To test Levine he asked, 'Then where are your wings?'

The Negro blushed as well as he was able. Manischevitz understood this from his changed expression. 'Under certain circumstances we lose privileges and prerogatives upon returning to
earth, no matter for what purpose, or endeavouring to assist
whosoever.'

'So tell me,' Manischevitz said, triumphantly, 'how did you get
get here?'

'I was transmitted.'

Still troubled, the tailor said, 'If you are a Jew, say the blessing
for bread.'

Levine recited it in sonorous Hebrew.

Although moved by the familiar words Manischevitz still felt
doubt that he was dealing with an angel.

'If you are an angel,' he demanded somewhat angrily, 'give me the
proof.'

Levine wet his lips. 'Frankly, I cannot perform either miracles
or near miracles, due to the fact that I am in a condition of proba-
tion. How long that will persist or even consist, I admit, depends on
the outcome.'

Manischevitz was racking his brains for some means of causing
Levine positively to reveal his true identity, when the Negro spoke
again:

'It was given me to understand that both your wife and you
require assistance of a salubrious nature?'

The tailor could not rid himself of the feeling that he was the butt
of a jokester. Is this what a Jewish angel looks like? he asked himself. This I am not convinced.

He asked a last question. 'So if God sends to me an angel, why a
black? Why not a white that there are so many of them?'

'It was my turn to go next,' Levine explained.

Manischevitz could not be persuaded. 'I think you are a faker.'

Levine slowly rose. His eyes showed disappointment and worry.
'Mr Manischevitz,' he said tonelessly, 'if you should desire me to be
of assistance to you any time in the near future, or possibly before,
I can be found' – he glanced at his fingernails – 'in Harlem.'

He was by then gone.

The next day Manischevitz felt some relief from his backache
and was able to work four hours at pressing. The day after, he put
in six hours; and the third day four again. Fanny sat up a little
and asked for some halvah to suck. But on the fourth day the
stabbing, breaking ache afflicted his back, and Fanny again lay
supine, breathing with blue-lipped difficulty.

Manischevitz was profoundly disappointed at the return of his
active pain and suffering. He had hoped for a longer interval of
easement, long enough to have some thought other than of himself
and his troubles. Day by day, hour by hour, minute after minute, he
lived in pain, pain his only memory, questioning the necessity of it,

inveighing against it, also, though with affection, against God. Why *so much*, Gottenyu? If he wanted to teach His servant a lesson for some reason, some cause – the nature of His nature – to teach him, say, for reasons of his weakness, his pride, perhaps, during his years of prosperity, his frequent neglect of God – to give him a little lesson, why then any of the tragedies that had happened to him, any *one* would have sufficed to chasten him. But *all together* – the loss of both his children, his means of livelihood, Fanny's health and his – that was too much to ask one frail-boned man to endure. Who, after all, was Manischevitz that he had been given so much to suffer? A tailor. Certainly not a man of talent. Upon him suffering was largely wasted. It went nowhere, into nothing: into more suffering. His pain did not earn him bread, nor fill the cracks in the wall, nor lift, in the middle of the night, the kitchen table; only lay upon him, sleepless, so sharply oppressively that he could many times have cried out yet not heard himself through this thickness of misery.

In this mood he gave no thought to Mr Alexander Levine, but at moments when the pain wavered, slightly diminishing, he sometimes wondered if he had been mistaken to dismiss him. A black Jew and angel to boot – very hard to believe, but suppose he *had* been sent to succour him, and he, Manischevitz, was in his blindness too blind to comprehend? It was this thought that put him on the knife-point of agony.

Therefore the tailor, after much self-questioning and continuing doubt, decided he would seek the self-styled angel in Harlem. Of course he had great difficulty, because he had not asked for specific directions, and movement was tedious to him. The subway took him to 116th Street, and from there he wandered in the dark world. It was vast and its lights lit nothing. Everywhere were shadows, often moving. Manischevitz hobbled along with the aid of a cane, and not knowing where to seek in the blackened tenement buildings, looked fruitlessly through store windows. In the stores he saw people and *everybody* was black. It was an amazing thing to observe. When he was too tired, too unhappy to go farther, Manischevitz stopped in front of a tailor's store. Out of familiarity with the appearance of it, with some sadness he entered. The tailor, an old skinny Negro with a mop of woolly grey hair, was sitting cross-legged on his workbench, sewing a pair of full-dress pants that had a razor slit all the way down the seat.

'You'll excuse me, please, gentleman,' said Manischevitz, admiring the tailor's deft, thimbled fingerwork, 'but you know maybe somebody by the name of Alexander Levine?'

The tailor, who Manischevitz thought, seemed a little antagonistic to him, scratched his scalp.

'Cain't say I ever heard dat name.'

'Alex-ander Lev-ine,' Manischevitz repeated it.

The man shook his head. 'Cain't say I heared.'

About to depart, Manischevitz remembered to say: 'He is an angel, maybe.'

'Oh *him*,' said the tailor clucking. 'He hang out in dat honky tonk down here a ways.' He pointed with his skinny finger and returned to the pants.

Manischevitz crossed the street against a red light and was almost run down by a taxi. On the block after the next, the sixth store from the corner was a cabaret, and the name in sparkling lights was Bella's. Ashamed to go in, Manischevitz gazed through the neon-lit window, and when the dancing couples had parted and drifted away, he discovered at a table on the side, towards the rear, Levine.

He was sitting alone, a cigarette butt hanging from the corner of his mouth, playing solitaire with a dirty pack of cards, and Manischevitz felt a touch of pity for him, for Levine had deteriorated in appearance. His derby was dented and had a grey smudge on the side. His ill-fitting suit was shabbier, as if he had been sleeping in it. His shoes and trouser cuffs were muddy, and his face was covered with an impenetrable stubble the colour of liquorice. Manischevitz, though deeply disappointed, was about to enter, when a big-breasted Negress in a purple evening gown appeared before Levine's table, and with much laughter through many white teeth, broke into a vigorous shimmy. Levine looked straight at Manischevitz with a haunted expression, but the tailor was too paralysed to move or acknowledge it. As Bella's gyrations continued, Levine rose, his eyes lit in excitement. She embraced him with vigour, both his hands clasped around her big restless buttocks and they tangoed together across the floor, loudly applauded by the noisy customers. She seemed to have lifted Levine off his feet and his large shoes hung limp as they danced. They slid past the windows where Manischevitz, white-faced, stood staring in. Levine winked slyly and the tailor left for home.

Fanny lay at death's door. Through shrunken lips she muttered concerning her childhood, the sorrows of the marriage bed, the loss of her children, yet wept to live. Manischevitz tried not to listen, but even without ears he would have heard. It was not a gift. The doctor panted up the stairs, a broad but bland, unshaven man (it was Sunday) and soon shook his head. A day at most, or two. He left at once, not without pity, to spare himself Manischevitz's multiplied sorrow; the man who never stopped hurting. He would someday get him into a public home.

Manischevitz visited a synagogue and there spoke to God, but God had absented himself. The tailor searched his heart and found no hope. When she died he would live dead. He considered taking his life although he knew he wouldn't. Yet it was something to consid r. Considering, you existed. He railed against God – Can you love a rock, a broom, an emptiness? Baring his chest, he smote the naked bones, cursing himself for having believed.

Asleep in a chair that afternoon, he dreamed of Levine. He was standing before a faded mirror, preening small decaying opalescent wings. 'This means,' mumbled Manischevitz, as he broke out of sleep, 'that it is possible he could be an angel.' Begging a neighbour lady to look in on Fanny and occasionally wet her lips with a few drops of water, he drew on his thin coat, gripped his walking stick, exchanged some pennies for a subway token, and rode to Harlem. He knew this act was the last desperate one of his woe: to go without belief, seeking a black magician to restore his wife to invalidism. Yet if there was no choice, he did at least what was chosen.

He hobbled to Bella's but the place had changed hands. It was now, as he breathed, a synagogue in a store. In the front, towards him, were several rows of empty wooden benches. In the rear stood the Ark, its portals of rough wood covered with rainbows of sequins; under it a long table on which lay the sacred scroll unrolled, illuminated by the dim light from a bulb on a chain overhead. Around the table, as if frozen to it and the scroll which they all touched with their fingers, sat four Negroes wearing skullcaps. Now as they read the Holy Word, Manischevitz could, through the plate-glass window, hear the singsong chant of their voices. One of them was old, with a grey beard. One was bubble-eyed. One was hump-backed. The fourth was a boy, no older than thirteen. Their heads moved in rhythmic swaying. Touched by this sight from his childhood and youth, Manischevitz entered and stood silent in the rear.

'Neshoma,' said bubble eyes, pointing to the word with a stubby finger. 'Now what dat mean?'

'That's the word that means soul,' said the boy. He wore glasses.

'Let's git on wid de commentary,' said the old man.

'Ain't necessary,' said the humpback. 'Souls is immaterial substance. That's all. The soul is derived in that manner. The immateriality is derived from the substance, and they both, causally an' otherwise, derived from the soul. There can be no higher.'

'That's the highest.'

'Over de top.'

'Wait a minute,' said bubble eyes. 'I don't see what is dat immaterial substance. How come de one gits hitched up to de odder?' He addressed the humpback.

'Ask me something hard. Because it is substanceless immateriality. It couldn't be closer together, like all the parts of the body under one skin – closer.'

'Hear now,' said the old man.

'All you done is switched de words.'

'It's the primum mobile, the substanceless substance from which comes all things that were incepted in the idea – you, me and everything and body else.'

'Now how did all dat happen? Make it sound simple.'

'It de speerit,' said the old man. 'On de face of de water moved

ABOVE and OPPOSITE ABOVE Typical scenes in Harlem, the poor Black quarter of New York

OPPOSITE CENTRE Boys of the Ethiopian Hebrew Congregation, the first Black Jewish sect in America, founded in 1921

OPPOSITE BELOW Rabbi W. A. Matthews of the Ethiopian Hebrew Congregation with a *bar mitzvah* boy

de speerit. An' dat was good. It say so in de Book. From de speerit ariz de man.'

'But now listen here. How come it become substance if it all de time a spirit?'

'God alone done dat.'

'Holy! Holy! Praise His Name.'

'But has dis spirit got some kind of a shade or colour?' asked bubble eyes, deadpan.

'Man of course not. A spirit is a spirit.'

'Then how come we is coloured?' he said with a triumphant glare.

'Ain't got nothing to do wid dat.'

'I still like to know.'

'God put the spirit in all things,' answered the boy. 'He put it in the green leaves and the yellow flowers. He put it with the gold in the fishes and the blue in the sky. That's how come it came to us.'

'Amen.'

'Praise Lawd and utter loud His speechless name.'

'Blow de bugle till it bust the sky.'

They fell silent, intent upon the next word. Manischevitz approached them.

'You'll excuse me,' he said. 'I am looking for Alexander Levine. You know him maybe?'

'That's the angel,' said the boy.

'Oh, *him*,' snuffed bubble eyes.

'You'll find him at Bella's. It's the establishment right across the street,' the humpback said.

Manischevitz said he was sorry that he could not stay, thanked them, and limped across the street. It was already night. The city was dark and he could barely find his way.

But Bella's was bursting with the blues. Through the window Manischevitz recognized the dancing crowd and among them sought Levine. He was sitting loose-lipped at Bella's side table. They were tippling from an almost empty whisky fifth. Levine had shed his old clothes, wore a shiny new chequered suit, pearl-grey derby, cigar, and big, two-tone button shoes. To the tailor's dismay, a drunken look had settled upon his formerly dignified face. He leaned towards Bella, tickled her ear lobe with his pinky, while whispering words that sent her into gales of raucous laughter. She fondled his knee. Manischevitz, girding himself, pushed open the door and was not welcomed.

'This place reserved.'

'Beat it, pale puss.'

'Exit, Yankel, Semitic trash.'

But he moved towards the table where Levine sat, the crowd breaking before him as he hobbled forward.

'Mr Levine,' he spoke in a trembly voice. 'Is here Manischevitz.'

Levine glared blearily. 'Speak yo' piece, son.'

Manischevitz shuddered. His back plagued him. Cold tremors tormented his crooked legs. He looked around, everybody was all ears.

'You'll excuse me. I would like to talk to you in a private place.'

'Speak. Ah is a private pusson.'

Bella laughed piercingly. 'Stop it, boy, you killin' me.'

Manischevitz, no end disturbed, considered fleeing but Levine addressed him:

'Kindly state the purpose of yo' communication with yo's truly.'

The tailor wet cracked lips. 'You are Jewish. This I am sure.'

Levine rose, nostrils flaring. 'Anythin' else yo' got to say?'

Manischevitz's tongue lay like stone.

'Speak now or fo'ever hold off.'

Tears blinded the tailor's eyes. Was ever man so tried? Should he say he believed a half-drunken Negro to be an angel?

The silence slowly petrified.

Manischevitz was recalling scenes of his youth as a wheel in his mind whirred: believe, do not, yes, no, yes, no. The pointer pointed to yes, to between yes and no, to no, no it was yes. He sighed. It moved but one had still to make a choice.

'I think you are an angel from God.' He said it in a broken voice, thinking, If you said it it was said. If you believed it you must say it. If you believed, you believed.

The hush broke. Everybody talked but the music began and they went on dancing. Bella, grown bored, picked up the cards and dealt herself a hand.

Levine burst into tears. 'How you have humiliated me.'

Manischevitz apologized.

'Wait'll I freshen up.' Levine went to the men's room and returned in his old clothes. No one said goodbye as they left.

They rode to the flat via subway. As they walked up the stairs Manischevitz pointed with his cane at his door.

'That's all been taken care of,' Levine said. 'You best go in while I take off.'

Disappointed that it was so soon over but torn by curiosity, Manischevitz followed the angel up three flights to the roof. When he got there the door was already padlocked.

Luckily he could see through a small broken window. He heard an odd noise, as though of a whirring of wings, and when he strained for a wider view, could have sworn he saw a dark figure borne aloft on a pair of magnificent black wings. A feather drifted down. Manischevitz gasped as it turned white, but it was only snowing.

He rushed downstairs. In the flat Fanny wielded a dust mop under the bed and then upon the cobwebs on the wall.

'A wonderful thing, Fanny,' Manischevitz said. 'Believe me, there are Jews everywhere.'

BERNARD MALAMUD

בני ישראל עשו כדבר משה וישאלו ממצרים כלי כסף וכלי זהב ושמלות

The Philosophers' Way

If religion is revealed by God, and God can be served by obeying His commandments, and sought by following the mystical path, what need is there of the human intellect to apply itself to Him? Philosophy is the attempt to understand the meaning of existence by means of the intellect. How, therefore, can there be such a thing as Jewish philosophy? It is true that some rabbis regarded philosophy with suspicion, apprehensive in case such a study, which they looked on as alien, should turn the scholar away from the God of his fathers. However, there were always Jews who saw this as a narrow approach, and believed that God could also be understood through an intellectual approach. It was the intention of these men to show how philosophy could be reconciled with Judaism, and in doing so they created a philosophical tradition which is specifically Jewish.

ABOVE Plato, whose ideas strongly influenced many Jewish philosophers

OPPOSITE ABOVE Jacob deceiving his blind father, Isaac, by impersonating his elder brother. This was one of the biblical stories which Philo insisted must be read allegorically before it could be understood

OPPOSITE BELOW Killing the Egyptian firstborn, the final plague before the Jews were allowed to leave Egypt

The Nature of Jewish Philosophy

Philosophy, from its original meaning of the love of knowledge, has come in time to mean the systematic study of the basic questions surrounding human existence and knowledge. The philosopher asks: is there a God? Is there anything that we can know with certainty? What is it to be good? And so on.

Judaism itself gives answers to these questions, but it does not follow that Judaism is a philosophical system. This is because philosophers have always tried to discover truth by means of *reason*; in other words, they have relied on the unaided efforts of the human mind. But Judaism has found its truth in *revelation*, in the words of God to man, recorded in the Bible. Religious Jews believe that greater certainty attaches to what we have learned from God than to anything we could learn from man alone. And for this reason they have not been driven to philosophy in the search for truth. Instead they have, for the most part, turned to the task of interpreting the Bible and deriving from it legal, moral and mystical knowledge, much of which is stored in those great repositories of biblical interpretation – the Talmud, the Midrash and the Zohar.

Despite this, however, there have been Jews in many periods of our history who have devoted themselves to philosophizing, and there is a large body of writing which we call Jewish philosophy. There is a special reason for this. Living as a minority group in a predominantly non-Jewish society, Jews have had to adjust to cultures that were not their own. This has frequently meant that they have encountered ideas different from, or even incompatible with, what they had learnt from the Bible and Jewish tradition. These encounters sometimes demanded a defence and this often resulted in fresh ways of looking at Judaism, new insights and emphases. It is the product of these encounters that we call Jewish philosophy. Jewish philosophy is not a simple search for truth as such, but rather the attempt to reconcile Judaism with other cultures. This does not mean that its achievements have been merely defensive. It is through the work of the great Jewish philosophers that Judaism has been kept perpetually up-to-date, rarely allowed to grow outmoded or irrelevant. They have seen it through a series of new eyes, and given it a succession of rebirths.

Philo

The first important Jewish philosopher was Philo Judaeus, who was born in Alexandria about 20 CE, and died some sixty years later. The Alexandrian Jewish community was, in his time, deeply influenced by the Greek language and culture. Philo's own family was of considerable social standing, and he had on the one hand assimilated a great deal of Greek philosophy and literature, while on the other he remained a firmly committed Jew, leading a delegation to the Emperor Caligula to protest against mistreatment of the Jewish community, and making a pilgrimage to the Temple at Jerusalem. He was a man of two cultures, and his philosophical efforts were directed towards harmonizing them. But how was he to reconcile two such different systems of thought as Greek philosophy, with its emphasis on abstract thought and contemplation, and Judaism, with its concrete picture of God as a person, and its insistence on a life of action? Philo's solution was to use the method of *allegory*. That is to say, by following up hints or nuances in the Bible, it can be read in a way that differs considerably from its usual, superficial sense. According to Philo, there are two ways of interpreting the Bible: the literal and the allegorical. And the allegorical meaning that Philo discovered in it turned out to be none other than a system of ideas akin to Greek philosophy. Philo was suggesting, in other words, that we only think that Greek and Jewish ideas are incompatible because we read the Bible in the wrong way.

The fundamental problem which Philo attempts to solve is this: how could an infinite God, who far surpasses our understanding, have created a finite material world? What relation could there be between two such different kinds of being? The fact that this is a problem for Philo shows us, incidentally, that he is a long way from seeing God as a *person*. The Bible speaks of God as if He had emotions (anger and compassion, for example) and as if He did things in the world (like dividing the Red Sea, or killing the Egyptian firstborn). Since, according to Philo, we must not suppose that God is directly involved in the world, but is *transcendent*, that is to say, He is infinitely aloof from and beyond the world, these passages must be read differently.

OPPOSITE A page from the *Mishneh Torah* by Moses Maimonides, perhaps the most influential of Jewish philosophers

פעמי
הבן כאמרתן ואל תשלטב
כל און

ספר חמשי והוא ספר קדוש

The answer that the Bible gives to the question: how could a God who transcends the universe have created it? is that God *spoke* and the world came into being. He said, let there be light, and there was light. So Philo develops this idea, that what relates the world to God is the *word* (or, in Greek, logos) which brings things into existence. This concept – logos – is a very complex one. Let us think of the word 'table'. What is the relation between this word and an actual table? We might say, the word contains or suggests the *idea* of a table. An idea is obviously more imperishable than a physical object – you can destroy a table but not the idea of one. So, when we talk about it in the context of the creation, the logos represents the *idea* of the world: like the world in that it has a definite form, and like God in that it is timeless and indestructible. But in addition, the logos actually brought the world into being. When God spoke, the world was created. Whereas when we say 'table' a table does not suddenly materialize. So logos is not simply an idea, it is also a *power* – the power which turns ideas into actuality. Philo maintains that the logos, which is part of God, is present and active at all times and in all places. To this extent he is a mystic. Everything in the world points to something beyond it.

We might, in the light of this, have expected Philo to be uninterested in *halakhah* (Jewish law), which is concerned with acting in certain ways, while he is more interested in contemplation. But surprisingly, this is not so. Philo was a strong believer in behaving according to the *halakhah*. He says, in effect, that our actions in keeping the Sabbath or celebrating the festivals may have symbolic meaning, but we should not, for that reason, care only about the meaning and forget about the practice.

The Medieval Period: Moses Maimonides

Philo's ideas were in time assimilated into Judaism, especially into Jewish mysticism, but their direct influence was small. No great philosophers emerged to develop his ideas, and it was not until the Middle Ages that Jewish philosophy reached its real flowering.

Here again it was the encounter with Greek ideas that provoked Jews to philosophize, though this time it was at one remove. The great period of Greek thought had long since ended, but its influence was transmitted to the Arab world, and reached especially the Jews in Spain, which was under Arab rule from the eighth century. One philosopher in particular, Aristotle, continued to be studied, by means of Arabic translations. Many medieval Jewish philosophers, like Ibn Daud, Gersonides and Maimonides were strongly influenced by him. The work of the other great pillar of Greek thought, Plato, also reached the Arabic world of that period through translations and the works of his followers. The Jews whose thought owes much to Plato include Ibn Gabirol, Bahya ibn Pakuda and

A page from Maimonides' *Guide to the the Perplexed*

Judah Halevi. For the Jews of the tenth to the fourteenth century, Plato and Aristotle represented the highest achievements of purely human thought. Of course, where their doctrines conflicted with Judaism (as for example where Aristotle holds that matter had existed for eternity while Judaism insists that the universe was created at a given moment in time) they were not followed. But for the most part what they had written was regarded as compatible with Judaism. The (for the most part Spanish) Jews of this period studied philosophy as earlier Jews had studied astronomy, as an *extension* of Judaism not as a challenge to it, a way of using man's powers of reasoning more fully to understand the marvels of God and the world. Never again were Jewish and non-Jewish philosophy to be so close to one another in their aims and methods.

The father of medieval Jewish philosophy was Sa'adya Gaon

(892–942), but indisputably the greatest was Moses Maimonides, born in Cordova, Spain, in 1135, who spent most of his adult life in Egypt, dying there in 1204. So highly was he regarded that he was called 'the second Moses'. The Jewish community in Spain at that time combined Jewish and secular learning to a rare degree. Though Maimonides' first works were almost entirely devoted to Jewish law, they already showed an awareness of philosophical problems and a tendency towards systematization that is characteristic of a mind steeped in the discipline of logic.

Maimonides' great philosophical work, written between 1180 and 1190, was the Guide to the Perplexed. The 'perplexed' for whom it was intended were those who were acquainted both with Jewish learning and with the teachings of Aristotle, and who found difficulty in reconciling them. In particular, such Jews would find many passages in the Bible where God is portrayed in human terms hard to accept, as had Philo.

Maimonides was convinced that the philosophers' conception of God as incorporeal (that is, without any bodily attributes) was the correct one. His procedure was to treat the anthropomorphic passages in the Bible (those where God is depicted as a person) as metaphorical and not to be taken literally. Other philosophers had already preceded him in this approach. But Maimonides was original in making the incorporeality of God the centre of his system, one of the basic principles of the Jewish faith. Book One of his Guide is devoted to this.

Sometimes, like Philo, he treats the biblical text as an allegory, hinting at a deeper meaning, but primarily he regards a word as a *homonym*, one word often having two quite separate meanings, like 'light' which means 'not heavy' or 'not dark'. 'Merciful', says Maimonides, is another homonym. It means one thing when applied to man, and another when applied to God. Likewise, when men are said in the Bible to 'see' God, this does not refer to physical sight, but to understanding, something perceived by the intellect rather than the eye. When God says to Moses, 'You cannot see My face', He means: no man can understand God in His *essence* (that is, as He is in Himself), but only by His works (that is, the things He does). Maimonides' point is that, though the Bible often uses the same words to describe God and man, the words mean different things in the two cases, and we cannot suppose that God has human characteristics.

One mistake that Maimonides warns us against is that of thinking that God's attributes are part of His essence. God is merciful and just, but this does not mean that He is *two things*, because, as the Bible tells us, God is One. It follows that His mercy and justice are not part of His essence (which is a unity), and this in turn leads us to conclude that in knowing that God is merciful, we have not yet reached the essential knowledge of God. Indeed, we can never reach this understanding.

How, then, do we have knowledge of God? Maimonides answers: only by knowing what He is not, not what He is. All that we can understand is that He exists, that He is not a plurality of things, that He is unlike any of the things He has created, and that nothing is beyond His power. Our knowledge of Him is purely negative. Any comparison between God and man is futile and heretical.

Maimonides then turns, in Book Two of the Guide, to the Aristotelian theory of the eternity of matter. This presents a difficulty to Jewish belief, because if some physical substance has always existed, the story of creation contained in the book of Genesis must be false because it suggests that the universe was created at a given moment in time, and before then there was no physical matter. The theory also posits the existence of something besides God which is eternal. Maimonides argues that the Aristotelians have not proved their case. Their arguments, and Maimonides' counter-arguments, are complex. But to take a simplified example: we might say that for something to come into being there has to be something which existed previously, to produce it. For a child to be born, its parents must have existed beforehand, and for them to have existed, they must have had parents before them, and so on. Therefore, there can be no first thing, because for anything that

we regard as the first, something had to exist before it to have brought it into being. And if the universe has no first point and no beginning, it must be eternal. Against this, Maimonides would argue that although as the universe *now* is, everything must have something which came before it, this law was itself created when God made the world. We cannot argue from the present to the infinite past, because this assumes an uninterrupted continuity of things happening as they do now. We know that this assumption is false, because at a certain point in time the world was created out of nothing, so that at one stage something came into being without anything physical existing before it.

Another problem which exercises Maimonides' attention is that of evil. How can a God who is good have created a world which contains evil? He answers that evil is not something which exists in its own right: it is simply the absence of good. In any case we cannot attribute any of the evil in the world to God. The evil which occurs is either inevitable, by virtue of the fact that man is a physical being, liable to disease and death; or it is caused by men, against other men (as in war) or against themselves (by letting themselves be led by their desires into too much eating, drinking or striving after love or wealth).

Finally Maimonides discusses the ethical life and the purpose of God's commandments. Often, he tries to give rational explanations for biblical commands which are difficult to understand. For example, he says that the real purpose of the sacrifices lay in the prayers which accompanied them. The sacrifices themselves were only a concession to the Israelites, who were still then spiritually immature and might otherwise have turned to idolatry. Likewise the prohibition of boiling meat in milk was intended to keep them far from similar heathen practices. Why, then, if we are no longer tempted to worship idols, do we continue to keep many of these laws? The reason, says Maimonides, is that God's laws must be definite, general and unconditional. They could not vary according to time and place without becoming uncertain and indefinite.

Maimonides' philosophy has not always been accepted in its totality by all Jews. But it has remained as one of the greatest achievements of Jewish thought, and it influenced many non-Jewish philosophers of the medieval period.

Judah Halevi

Coming before Maimonides in time, but best understood in contrast to him, is the poet and philosopher Judah Halevi (born around 1085 in Spain; died shortly after 1140). Like Maimonides, Halevi practised medicine, but unlike him his temperament was poetic rather than given to abstractions, and his poetry stands at the peak of the Jewish literature of the Middle Ages.

OPPOSITE ABOVE The former synagogue in Toledo, Spain, now a church. Toledo was the home of philosopher and poet Judah Halevi

OPPOSITE BELOW A plaque in the Toledo synagogue. In the Middle Ages, the Spanish Jewish community had many brilliant religious and secular scholars

Though we call him a philosopher, he was in fact opposed to the mainstream of the philosophy of his age. It seemed to him to place too much emphasis on thought as opposed to action, too much on highly general truths instead of the very specific beliefs of Judaism which apply only to Jews; and it seemed to lose sight of the uniqueness of Israel as the Jewish homeland. His love for Israel, which animated much of his poetry, finally impelled him to leave Spain on a pilgrimage to Jerusalem (for more about his journey, see pp. 160–1).

His major philosophical work is called the *Kuzari,* and it takes its name from the fact that it is written in the form of an imaginary dialogue between the king of the Khazars (a pagan), and a Jew whom he had asked to teach him the fundamentals of Judaism. The Khazars were a Caucasian people who had in large numbers converted to Judaism in the eighth century. Halevi imagines the kind of reasons which might have been put forward by Jews to convince them, and uses them to express his own ideas.

At the outset of the book he establishes his differences of opinion with the philosophers. He describes the king as having a dream in which he is told 'Your intentions are acceptable to God, but not your actions'. The king then summons a philosopher, to learn how to mend his ways, but he is told only a series of ideas about God and the world; and he wanted to change not his ideas but his behaviour. He then has conversations with a Christian and a Muslim, which still leave him unsatisfied. So he turns, in desperation, to a Jew. Immediately the Jew surprises him by saying that no certainty can ever come from a religion which is based on reason, because every argument can be met by counter-argument. Certainty is only to be found in a religion which rests on revelation, because this is something which is directly experienced and cannot be denied. And this is Judaism, because its law, the Torah, was given by God to Moses in the sight of the whole nation at Sinai, and has since been handed down by uninterrupted tradition.

This insistence on revelation as opposed to reason sets Judah Halevi in strong contrast to Maimonides. For Maimonides, the central belief of Judaism was a philosophical one: the existence of an incorporeal God, which can be proved by reason. But for Halevi, God is known through history, both in His revelations to Moses, the Patriarchs and the Prophets, and in His miraculous protection of the Jewish people. The highest knowledge of God comes not through philosophical proofs of His existence, but in the Divine word spoken to the prophets. It is this *direct* knowledge – communication from God – which is lacking in Greek thought and represents its failings.

Alongside his belief in the primacy of prophecy over other forms of knowledge, goes a belief in the primacy of Israel over other nations. God gave the commandments and the power of prophecy only to Israel; the land of Israel has a unique holiness; and the Hebrew language is unparalleled in its richness. Halevi's pride

BELOW The sacrifice of Isaac on a page from Maimonides' *Mishneh Torah*

OPPOSITE Letter from Hisdai ibn Shaprut of Spain to Joseph, king of the Khazars (10th century)

OPPOSITE BELOW A traditional portrait of Judah Halevi

in his people is not simple chauvinism. Israel may be more privileged, but it also bears a heavier responsibility: it is punished more severely for its sins, and it even suffers for the sins of other nations.

The commandments, which are binding only on Jews because of their special relation with God, cannot all be explained rationally. The important thing is not only to do them with the correct understanding and intention (though this, of course, is necessary) but to perform them according to all the details laid down in the law. In this Halevi is not only answering the king's original request, that he learn how to correct his behaviour rather than his intentions. He is also stressing that Judaism is primarily a religion which demands perfect action, not only, as the philosophers might lead us to believe, correctness in thought. The book ends, appropriately, with the imaginary Jewish spokesman taking his leave of the king, to set out, as Halevi himself did, to visit Jerusalem.

The *Kuzari* failed in its main intention, to rid Judaism of the excesses of philosophy. For almost as Halevi died, Maimonides was born to reinstate the use of reason. But it remains as a powerful statement of the opposing case, and it has influenced the most recent thinkers that we will be discussing, the Jewish existentialists.

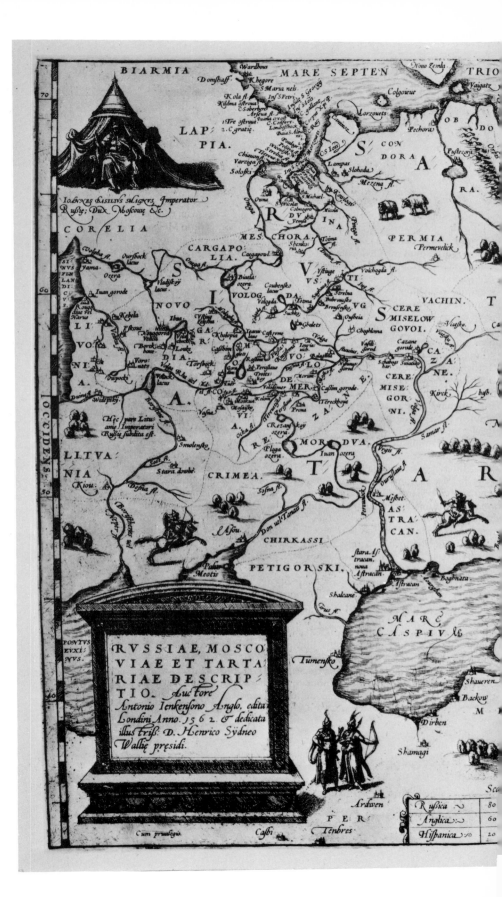

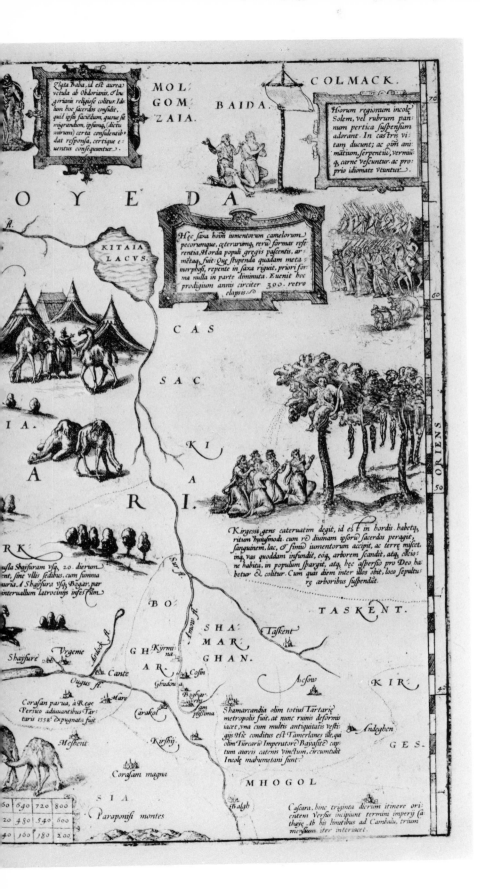

ZIçta Baba, id est aurea
vetula ab Oblorinis, & lou
gorianis reliquiße colitur. Ideo
Ian hoc sacerdos considit,
quæ ipsis faciedum, quove sū
migrandum, ipsumq, (dictu
mirum) certa consulentib'
dat responsa, certique e=
uentus consequuntur.

MOL GOM ZAIA.

BAIDA.

COLMACK.

Horum regionum incolę
Solem, vel rubrum pan=
num pertica suspensum
adorant. In castris vi=
tam ducunt; ac oīm ani
mātium, serpentiū, vermiū
q, carne vescuntur. ac pro=
prio idiomate vtuntur.

OYEDA

KITAIA LACVS.

Hęc saxa hoīm iumentorum camelorum
pecorumque, cęterarumq, rerū formas refe
rentia, Horda populi gregis pascentis, ar=
mētaq, fuit: Quę stupenda quadam meta=
morphosi, repente in saxa riguit, priori for=
ma nulla in parte diminuta. Euenit hoc
prodigium annis circiter 300. retro
elapsis.

CAS

SAC

KI A RI.

*Kirgessi gens cateruatim degit, id est in hordis habetq,
ritum hausmodi cum rē diuinam ipsoru sacerdos peragit,
sanguinem, lac, & simū iumentorum accipit, ac terrę miscet,
inq, vas quoddam infundit, eoq, arborem scandit, atq, cōcio=
ne habita, in populum spargit, atq, hęc aspersio pro Deo ha=
betur & colitur. Cum quas diem inter illos obit, loco sepultu=
rę arboribus suspendit.*

ustra Shaysuram vsq. 20. dierum
ent, sine vllis sedibus, cum summa
auria. A Shaysura vsq, Bogar, par
interuallum latrocinijs infestum

BO

GHAR=

SHA MAR GHAN.

Kyrmi na

Taskent

TASKENT.

KIR=

GES.

Shaysurē   Vrgeme
Cante
Oigus fl.
Ghudou a
Boghar vehs
tam plißima
Cosin
Ascsow
Andeghen

Corasan parua, à Rege
Persico adiuuantibus Tar=
taris 1558 expugnata fuit

Carakol
Mare
Kirshij

Shamarcandia olim totius Tartarię
metropolis fuit, at nunc ruinis deformis
iacet, vna cum multis antiquitatis vesti=
gijs Hic conditus est Tamerlanes ille, qui
olim Türcarū Imperatorē Bayasitē cap
tum aureis catenis vinctum, circumtulit
Incolę mahumetani sunt.

Meshent

MHOGOL

SIA

Paraponisi montes

Balgh

Cascara, hinc triginta dierum itinere ori=
entem Versus incipiunt termini imperij (a=
thaye sib his limitibus ad Cambalu, trium
mensium iter interiacet.

560	640	720	800
20	480	540	600
40	160	180	200

The Emancipation: Moses Mendelssohn

Jewish philosophy was almost silent for over three hundred years after the death of Albo, the last great thinker of the Middle Ages. These were years of persecution and suffering, a time when Jews were herded together behind ghetto walls and had no desire or opportunity to come to terms with the contemporary non-Jewish culture. They were shut off from it, and they turned inwards to the labyrinths of Jewish law without looking beyond. Then, beginning in the middle of the eighteenth century, social and intellectual freedom became again a possibility, and Jewish philosophy was reborn. The date was 1783, the place was Berlin, and the man was Moses Mendelssohn.

Philosophy, at that time, had a more urgent task than it had had at the time of Maimonides. Then, it had surfaced in a Jewish community already well-versed in other cultures; now it was to be written at a period when much of the Jewish world was culturally in the Middle Ages. Mendelssohn had to open its eyes to a wider world.

He was born in Dessau in 1729, but moved to Berlin when he was thirteen, to pursue his studies, and he died there in 1786. In Berlin he studied, as well as Talmud, mathematics and Latin and acquired a gift for German prose writing. In 1767 he wrote a book on the immortality of the soul, called *Phaedon*, which brought him into prominence in the literary circles of his day. Soon afterwards a preacher from Zurich, named Lavater, made a public attempt to convert Mendelssohn to Christianity, inviting him either to prove that Christianity was false, or else to adopt it as his own faith. This was a real dilemma. Mendelssohn was an advocate of religious tolerance. He neither wished to give up his Judaism nor did he want to give offence by criticizing Christianity. He wrote a disarming reply, but the controversy and its repercussions forced him to reassess his religious position, and to defend the combination of firm Jewish commitment with tolerance towards other religions.

The most important result of this rethinking was his book *Jerusalem*, published in 1783. In it he argued for a separation of the Church and the State. In other words, no religious body should be allowed the right to pass laws which excluded a man from any right simply on the basis of his religious conviction. Just as a doctor treats a patient without regard for his beliefs, so should a judge not treat two men differently because they hold different religious views. The state is concerned with the relations between man and man, whereas religion is concerned with the relation between man and God. Their interests can never conflict because God needs nothing from man. The objectives of Church and State, and their fields of authority, are therefore entirely separate.

So far this is political, rather than religious, philosophy. But

Berlin in the 18th century

Moses Mendelssohn

Mendelssohn then goes on to propose a novel interpretation of Judaism to support his argument. Surely Judaism involves the very thing that Mendelssohn wanted to deny, namely the right to punish a man for holding false (that is, heretical) beliefs? No, says Mendelssohn. Judaism is not revealed *religion* but revealed *legislation*. When God issued His commandments on Sinai, He did not say, '*Believe* this and not that.' He said, '*Do* this and not that.' The only beliefs that Judaism involves are those that any man could arrive at by reason. He therefore maintained that Judaism exercises no religious intolerance in the realm of thought. Its essence lies in a certain way of *acting*, in accordance with the Divine command.

Although Mendelssohn's main intention was a relatively narrow one – to argue against the restrictions imposed on Jews attaining citizenship and employment in the service of the state, the effect of his work was to liberate Jews from any curtailment of their free thought in the name of Judaism. This had consequences, namely the weakening of Jewish practice itself as Jews became steadily more influenced by German values.

The Reform Movement and the Science of Judaism

Following the lead given unwittingly by Mendelssohn, a movement arose in Germany at the beginning of the nineteenth century to change the very character of Judaism. Mendelssohn had opened the way to an involvement with German culture. But two things stood in the way of Jewish integration with German life. One was the belief in Jewish nationhood, the idea that in the Messianic future Jews would again inhabit Israel as a holy people in a holy land. This meant that they would have to regard their stay in any country of exile, like Germany, as only temporary and provisional, and this prevented them from making themselves at home there. The second obstacle was the fact that many Jewish laws inevitably set Jews socially apart: they could not eat the same food as their non-Jewish friends, they could not work on the Sabbath and so on. It seemed to follow that the only way to achieve social integration was to eliminate these elements from Judaism. This was, of course, precisely what Mendelssohn was opposed to – the reform of Jewish law. But the pressure for these changes was strong, and out of it the Reform Movement was born.

As was to be expected, the reforms consisted in removing all references to the Messiah, and to supposedly outmoded practices like sacrifice, from the prayerbook; changing aspects of synagogue ritual; and ceasing to apply many of the laws which barred the Jews from integration into German life.

Underlying these practical changes was a philosophical position. The Reform Movement looked to the present rather than the past. They wished to make themselves at home in exile, not eternally looking backwards to Sinai or forward to the Messiah. They had to show that Judaism allowed radical change to accommodate to the needs of the moment.

One impetus to this search for a philosophy came from the historical researches of Zunz and Geiger, a study known as the Science of Judaism. They were able to show that Judaism had not been static but has undergone continuous change. The Talmud does not simply express the Bible in greater detail – it goes beyond it in many ways. If it could innovate changes, why could not the Jews of nineteenth-century Germany? Zunz himself did not conclude that drastic reforms were justified, but Geiger was convinced that a change must be made in favour of the spirit as against the letter of the law. We can distinguish between Jewish laws which are moral, applying universally between man and man, and those which are specific to the relation between Jews and their God. The latter were now considered outmoded, for the task of Jews was no longer to live as people apart, but to participate in the universal betterment of mankind.

Naturally the movement met with strong opposition from Orthodox Jews, most forcefully in the person of Samson Raphael Hirsch. His task was to restate traditional Judaism in contemporary terms, to show that the 'spirit' of the law could not be separated from its practice, and to demonstrate that the traditional Jew did not have to jettison his ancient religion to be able to enter fully into German life. He pointed out that Torah does not mean 'law' but 'teaching', and that Jews are charged with the duty of demonstrating the truths of its teaching by their way of life. The commandments are *symbols* of these truths, and therefore they must be performed with understanding and involvement if their symbolic character is not to be lost. But the spirit which they embody can only be achieved by practising them. Therefore Judaism in its traditional form cannot be written off as lifeless law, nor can its spirit be discovered elsewhere than in its observance.

This process of adjusting Judaism to the demands of modernity has continued to the present day, and it has produced other movements – Conservative, Liberal and Reconstructionist. The debate continues, and no easy answers are to be found.

Leopold Zunz

Abraham Geiger

Jewish Existentialism: Buber and Rosenzweig

One movement of Jewish thought, specific to the twentieth century, cut across the lines of the practical controversy between Reform and Orthodox, and has significantly influenced the development of religious thinking in general. This is Jewish existentialism. Its major exponents were two friends who collaborated together in a translation of the Bible into German, Franz Rosenzweig (1886–1929) and Martin Buber (1878–1965). Their work is hard to summarize,

Martin Buber

Rosenzweig's because of its complexity, Buber's because he was so prolific and because his thought went through many transformations in his long life. But this much can be said: they were both attempting to break out of the rationalism which Mendelssohn had started in the modern era, and which Reform, and to some extent German orthodoxy, continued. They sought experience rather than abstraction. They wanted to *meet* God, not simply to contemplate Him. They wished to reinstate God as a person, as He is in the Bible, who speaks directly to man, in place of the 'God of the philosophers', an intellectual concept. They wanted to recover, in other words, all that German Jewry had for two hundred years regarded as primitive, but which they felt was the real life and vitality of Judaism.

Franz Rosenzweig

Their backgrounds, and therefore their ultimate directions, were very different. Buber came from a family long famous for its Jewish scholarship. Rosenzweig, on the other hand, came from an assimilated family. Several of his friends and relatives had converted to Christianity, and he was on the verge of it himself until the experience of an Atonement Day service in a small traditional synagogue in Berlin (1913) made him realize that his future lay within Judaism. His task was to discover Judaism afresh. His path was the way of return, precisely the opposite direction to the path which had led German Jewry out of the ghettos a century before. A tragically premature paralysis and death prevented him from completing it.

Both men found inspiration in the still unemancipated Jewry of Eastern Europe which retained its naïve vigour while other European Jews were acquiring a secular sophistication. Much of Buber's work consisted of translating the tales and legends of the Hasidim, the followers of the Baal Shem Tov (1700–1760). Hasidism, being a movement of the often unlearned Jewish masses, had produced an ability to speak to God in prayer almost as Abraham had once done – in the tones of conversation between one person and another. Alongside this went an insistence on *Ahavat Yisrael* – the collective love of Jews for one another and the refusal to despise another Jew for his ignorance or impiety. Buber has done much to bring their great body of folklore, in which these values were expressed, to the attention of the wider world (three such stories can be found in this book, on pages 55, 137 and 174). These two ideas, the love of man for a personal God, and the fellow-love amongst Jews, heavily influenced his most famous book, *I and Thou*. In it he draws a distinction between two kinds of relationship, the I-It relation in which the person is detached from the other: he knows him but is not involved with him; and the I-Thou relation, in which a person is absolutely open to the other, prepared to be changed by him, and regarding him with as much active concern as he has for himslef. Philosophy related to God in an I-It way, but religion *encounters* Him in an I-Thou meeting. This view takes us immediately back to the Bible, and indeed Buber spent much of his life trying to understand the religious experience which underlies the world of Moses and the Prophets. But he goes further in his suggestion (already hinted at in some Hasidic writers) that God is the universal Thou, or that we really meet God in our I-Thou relationships with other people. This implicit rejection of a God beyond the world and man takes Buber out of the realm of orthodox Jewish thought, and his writings have in fact been most influential amongst non-Jewish thinkers.

Rosenweig's great work, the *Star of Redemption*, was written on postcards in the trenches of World War I. It was written only three years after his decision not to convert to Christianity, and much of it is devoted to understanding the relation between Christianity and Judaism. Judaism, he says, is the eternal life; Christianity the eternal way. Or, taking the star as his symbol, Judaism is the fire at its centre, Christianity the rays which emanate from it. By this he means that the Jewish community lives, in a sense, apart from time. Its faith is handed on from one generation to the next; it lives within itself, not seeking to convert the world; it remains bound to the eternal teachings of the Torah and to the yearly cycle of the Jewish festivals which impose on it a pattern of time (half past, half future) quite separate from the progression of years in the secular calendar. But Christianity is not a faith preserved within a race. Every Christian must freely undertake commitment. It seeks to penetrate the world and make conversions. Timelessness does not belong to the community or its institutions, only to the individual in his relation to God.

This analysis is original in two ways. First, it does not try to defend Judaism against Christianity, or to point out the similarities between them, but to understand one in the light of the other. This is something which previous Jewish thinkers had not felt the need to do, or even thought of doing. It represents a new confidence in the ability of the Jew to discover new depths in his religion because of, and not despite, his involvement with other faiths. Second, it contrasts the two religions not in terms of their *beliefs*, but of their *experiences*. This is characteristic of the existentialist method.

New Directions

What had provoked and inspired these last two hundred years of philosophy had been the need to come to terms with non-Jewish values. Since then, three factors have supplanted this motivation. First was the Holocaust, with its ironic judgment on the assimilated German Jews. Second was the birth of the State of Israel in 1948. Jews now have a homeland, and this has added a complicating element to their loyalties, and made it necessary to rethink the purpose of Jewish existence in exile. Third, a large part of the Jewish world is estranged from its Judaism and needs less to learn to integrate with its non-Jewish neighbours than to rediscover its own culture and traditions. These facts suggest that the Jewish philosophy of the future will be more introspective, more concerned with discovering a Jewish identity, and more interested in reviving the forms of religious experience, than it has been in the past.

But we will continue to look to the philosophers for new directions. Their role will be what it has essentially always been, to build a bridge between the spiritual needs of the present and resources of the past. We need Jewish philosophy now as much as ever.

JONATHAN SACKS

The Man Who Slept
Through the End
of the World

He was always sleepy. And always ready to sleep. Everywhere. At the biggest mass meetings, at all the concerts, at every important convention, he could be seen sitting asleep.

And he slept in every conceivable and inconceivable pose. He slept with his elbows in the air and his hands behind his head. He slept standing up, leaning against himself so that he shouldn't fall down. He slept in the theatre, in the streets, in the synagogue. Wherever he went, his eyes would drip with sleep.

Neighbours used to say that he had already slept through seven big fires, and once, at a really big fire, he was carried out of his bed, still asleep, and put down on the sidewalk. In this way he slept for several hours until a patrol came along and took him away.

It was said that when he was standing under the wedding canopy and reciting the vows, 'Thou art to me . . .' he fell asleep at the word 'sanctified', and they had to beat him over the head with brass pestles for several hours to wake him up. And he slowly said the next word and again fell asleep.

We mention all this so that you may believe the following story about our hero.

Once, when he went to sleep, he slept and slept and slept; but in his sleep it seemed to him that he heard thunder in the streets and his bed was shaking somewhat; so he thought in his sleep that it was raining outside, and as a result his sleep became still more delicious. He wrapped himself up in his quilt and in his warmth.

When he awoke he saw a strange void: his wife was no longer there, his bed was no longer there, his quilt was no longer there. He wanted to look through the window, but there was no window to look through. He wanted to run down the three flights and yell,

'Help!' but there were no stairs to run on and no air to yell in. And when he wanted merely to go out of doors, he saw that there was no out of doors. Evaporated!

For a while he stood there in confusion, unable to comprehend what had happened. But afterward he bethought himself: I'll go to sleep. He saw, however, that there was no longer any earth to sleep on. Only then did he raise two fingers to his forehead and reflect: Apparently I've slept through the end of the world. Isn't that a fine how-do-you-do?

He became depressed. No more world, he thought. What will I do without a world? Where will I go to work, how will I make a living, especially now that the cost of living is so high and a dozen eggs costs a dollar twenty and who knows if they're even fresh, and besides, what will happen to the five dollars the gas company owes me? And where has my wife gone off to? Is it possible that she too has disappeared with the world, and with the thirty dollars' pay I had in my pockets? And she isn't by nature the kind that disappears, he thought to himself.

And what will I do if I want to sleep? What will I stretch out on if there isn't any world? And maybe my back will ache? And who'll finish the bundle of work in the shop? And suppose I want a glass of malted, where will I get it?

Eh, he thought, have you ever seen anything like it? A man should fall asleep with the world under his head and wake up without it!

As our hero stood there in his underwear, wondering what to do, a thought occurred to him: To hell with it! So there isn't any world! Who needs it anyway? Disappeared is disappeared: I might as well go to the movies and kill some time. But to his astonishment he saw that, together with the world, the movies had also disappeared.

A pretty mess I've made here, thought our hero, and began smoothing his moustache. A pretty mess I've made here, falling asleep! If I hadn't slept so soundly, he taunted himself, I would have disappeared along with everything else. This way I'm unfortunate, and where will I get a malted? I love a glass in the morning. And my wife? Who knows who she's disappeared with? If it's with that presser from the top floor, I'll murder her, so help me God.

Who knows how late it is?

With these words our hero wanted to look at his watch but couldn't find it. He searched with both hands in the left and right pockets of the infinite emptiness but could find nothing to touch.

I just paid two dollars for a watch and here it's already disappeared, he thought to himself. All right. If the world went under, it went under. That I don't care about. It isn't my world. But the watch! Why should my watch go under? A new watch. Two dollars. It wasn't even wound.

And where will I find a glass of malted?

He slept in every conceivable and inconceivable pose

There's nothing better in the morning than a glass of malted. And who knows if my wife . . . I've slept through such a terrible catastrophe, I deserve the worst. Help, help, h-e-e-lp! Where were my brains? Why didn't I keep an eye on the world and my wife? Why did I let them disappear when they were still so young?

And our hero began to beat his head against the void, but since the void was a very soft one it didn't hurt him and he remained alive to tell this story.

MOISHE NADIR translated by Irving Howe

The Defenders

Maintaining its identity, and even its very existence, has been a long, hard struggle for the Jewish people. Even while they still lived in Eretz Israel, their desire for independence was a political nuisance to the super-powers of the time. Later, dispersed throughout the world, they lived under the rule of societies whose own religion made them regard Judaism as, at best, a stubborn refusal to acknowledge God's truth and, at worst, an alliance with the devil. Attacks on Jews were therefore commonplace, an almost natural reaction to bad times. Contrary to what is sometimes believed, the Jews were not content to be passive sufferers. At different periods, and in different places, when the survival of the community was threatened, heroes and heroines arose to defend their people. The stories of a few of them are told below.

Bar Kokhba

On the ninth of the month of Av, 70 CE, a Roman torch set the Temple aflame. The orders of Titus, the Roman conqueror of Jerusalem, were explicit: to destroy the Temple, the last vestige of Jewish independence and the focal point of the ardent religious feelings of the Jews. A couple of weeks later the last defenders of the city, starved almost to death, were slain or taken into captivity by the Romans and Jerusalem was sacked. Thus, in streams of blood and devastating flames, the Great Revolt (or Jewish War) came to an end. Only the almost inaccessible stronghold of Masada, overlooking the Dead Sea, continued to resist the Roman legions until its heroic and tragic end three years later. The Romans had every right to believe that they had succeeded in breaking the rebellious spirit of the Jews; but subsequent events proved that they were mistaken. After barely sixty-two years had elapsed, the Jews in the land of Israel rose again in a sweeping revolt against their Roman oppressors, a revolt that was in many respects even more formidable, and certainly fiercer and more brutal than the Great Revolt. This was the Bar Kokhba revolt.

Who was this man whose name has drifted down to us across the stormy waves of so many centuries? Until a few years ago almost nothing was known about him apart from his name and a few vague legends. And even as regards his name there was no conformity of opinion, since in some sources he is called Bar Kokhba, and in others Bar Kosiba. No historian recorded the events of the Bar Kokhba uprising as Josephus Flavius, the Jewish historian and statesman, did the Jewish War. A few scattered references were all that remained.

Then, in 1952, only five years after the sensational discovery of

OPPOSITE Roman legionaries attack

the first Dead Sea scrolls, another astonishing discovery was made in the same area. Again it was Bedouins searching in one of the couple of thousand caves along the shores of the Dead Sea who found new papyri. When these papyri reached the hands of scholars the world was once more astonished. Here, over eighteen centuries later, were original letters dictated by Simeon Bar Kosiba. Thus, at last, the riddle of his name was solved. We now know that on the basis of his original name, Bar Kosiba (perhaps Kosiba was derived from his birth place or perhaps it was his father's name), he was called Bar Kokhba, 'Son of the Star', by his ardent followers, who regarded him as the King Messiah. Thus the Midrash tells us that when Rabbi Akiva beheld Bar Kosiba he exclaimed 'This is the King Messiah!' with reference to the biblical verse (Num. 24:17): 'There shall step forth a star (*kokhav*) out of Jacob.' On the other hand, his opponents called him Bar Kozivah, 'Son of the Liar', from *kazav*, the Hebrew word for 'lie'.

The immediate cause for the outbreak of Bar Kokhba's revolt seems to have been the intention of the Roman Emperor Hadrian to build a Roman colony, Aelia Capitolina, on the ruins of Jerusalem, and to build a temple to Jupiter on the site of the Temple. Such an outrage could not be tolerated by the Jewish people. The preparations for the revolt were quite extensive. Dio Cassius, the Roman historian in whose work an account of the war was preserved, tells us that the Jews 'purposely made of poor quality such weapons as they were called upon to furnish, in order that the Romans might reject them and they themselves might thus have

BELOW LEFT The bundle of letters written by Simeon bar Kosiba, just as they were found

BELOW Emperor Hadrian

the use of them'. They also 'occupied the advantageous positions in the country and strengthened them with mines and walls, in order that they might have places of refuge whenever they should be hard pressed, and might meet together unobserved under ground; and they pierced these subterranean passages from above at intervals to let the air and light in.'

The Midrash (Lamentations Rabbah) tells of the ferocity of Bar Kokhba and his soldiers, and also of their large number. As a test of fortitude Bar Kokhba ordered each recruit to cut off a finger, and so Bar Kokhba 'had with him two hundred thousand men with an amputated finger. The Sages sent him the message, "How long will you continue to make the men of Israel blemished?" He asked them, "How else shall they be tested?" They answered, "Let anyone who cannot uproot a cedar from Lebanon be refused enrolment in your army." He thereupon had two hundred thousand men of each class.'

The revolt broke out into the open in 132 CE. At that time two Roman legions were stationed in the land of Israel. Bar Kokhba and his warriors dealt a crushing blow to these legions. The whole of Judaea, including Jerusalem, and most of the other regions of Israel were liberated and Jewish rule instituted. In Jerusalem Hebrew inscriptions were stamped on Roman coins; many were inscribed '*Shimon nesi Yisrael*' (Simeon Prince of Israel), while others read 'Year one of the redemption of Israel' or 'Year two of the freedom of Israel'.

Meanwhile the Roman governor of Syria was dispatched to quell the rebellion, and legions from Egypt and Arabia were sent to reinforce his legions. But Bar Kokhba and his men fought so bravely and effectively that they defeated these forces as well, totally annihilating one of the legions from Egypt. Hadrian had no choice now but to send against the Jews his best general, Julius Severus. The Roman governor of faraway Britain was ordered to come at once, bringing with him not only his best legions but legions from the Danube provinces as well. Twelve legions in all took part in the war against Bar Kokhba.

At this stage of the war the Jews lost their grip on Galilee, and a most ferocious war was waged in Judaea, described in these terms by Dio Cassius: 'Severus did not venture to attack his opponents in the open at any one point, in view of their numbers and their desperation, but by intercepting small groups, thanks to the number of his soldiers and his under-officers and by depriving them of food and shutting them up, he was able, rather slowly, to be sure, but with comparatively little danger, to crush, exhaust and exterminate them.' In this manner Severus was able to capture one stronghold after the other, until at last, possibly after he had captured the unfortified Jerusalem, he trapped Bar Kokhba in his last stronghold, Bethar.

Bethar lies about seven miles south west of Jerusalem. At that

Roman legionary of Bar Kokhba's day

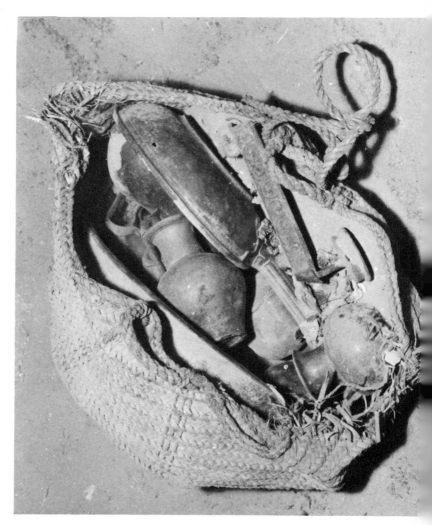

ABOVE Coins made during the Bar
Kokhba revolt

ABOVE RIGHT A heap of stone balls used
as ammunition in Roman catapults

RIGHT A woman's household utensils,
still intact centuries after her tragic death

OPPOSITE ABOVE Bar Kokhba's battle
orders

OPPOSITE One of Bar Kokhba's warriors

Objects found in the Judean Desert caves

time it was rather a large town, strongly fortified. Severus laid strict siege to Bethar. From time to time the defenders sallied out of the town in an effort to destroy the Roman siege machines. In the words of the legend, 'And what used Bar Kosiba to do? He would catch the missiles from the enemy's catapults on one of his knees and hurl them back, killing many of the foe.'

But hunger and thirst took their toll and after the siege had lasted a year Bar Kokhba and his men were at the end of their tether. Finally on the ninth of Av the Romans succeeded in breaking into the town: 'They slew the inhabitants until the horses waded in blood up to the nostrils, and the blood rolled along huge stones and flowed into the sea, staining it for a distance of four miles.' Bar Kokhba 'was slain and his head taken to Hadrian. "Who killed him?" asked Hadrian. A Cuthean said to him, "I killed him!" "Bring his body to me," Hadrian ordered. The Cuthean went and found a snake encircling its neck; so Hadrian when told of this exclaimed, "If his God had not slain him who could have overcome him?" '

According to Dio Cassius five hundred and eighty thousand Jews were killed in the various battles, and many others perished through famine or disease. The whole of Judaea was desolate. It was indeed a very cruel war, with many thousands of Romans killed as well. So much so, that when Hadrian announced his victory to the senate he did not dare to employ the time-hallowed formula of 'If you and your children are in health, it is well; I and the legions are in health'.

A few score of Jewish warriors managed to escape the massacre, and they and their families took refuge in the most secluded parts of the Judaean Desert. They hid themselves in caves, which could only be entered by means of ropes. Unable to attack the caves, the Romans blockaded the land around them, eventually starving the fugitives to death.

In 1960 an archaeological expedition led by Professor Yigael Yadin (a former chief-of-staff of the Israeli army) was closely examining some of these caves, which were situated in the midst of precipitous cliffs near the Dead Sea. Inch by inch the archaeologists unearthed the tragedy which had taken place in those caves more than eighteen hundred years before. Skulls and bones told the gruesome story. Then one day a heap of papyri was found hidden in a dark corner of one of the caves. When these papyri were carefully opened it turned out they were letters dictated by Bar Kokhba himself. Thus, eighteen centuries after it was dictated by the last 'chief-of-staff' of Judaea, another Jewish soldier, this time the chief-of-staff of the Israeli army, could read one of Bar Kokhba's commands:

Simeon Bar Kosiba to Yehonathan son of Be'ayan and to Masabala . . . get hold of the young men and come with them; if not – a punishment. And I shall deal with the Romans.

Dhu Nuwas

During the first centuries of the Christian era, there existed a flourishing kingdom in the south-western corner of Arabia: Himyar. Its inhabitants were mainly pagans, but there were also not a few Jews and some Christians living there. The kingdom of Himyar was a prosperous one, and being situated between the Indian Ocean and the Red Sea, it was also an important strategic point. It is easy to understand, then, why the Christian Byzantine Empire and the Sasanid kingdom of Persia were each trying to gain control over the independent Himyarite kingdom. The tools of Byzantium in the struggle were the Christian rulers of Ethiopia, while those of Persia were some Jewish envoys. The heathen kings of Himyar quickly understood that to become Christians would be to come under the supremacy of the Byzantine Empire. On the other hand, there was no independent Jewish state for them to fear. They therefore decided to convert to Judaism. An Arabian legend narrates what happened: first to convert was the king, who was persuaded to do so by two Jewish sages. He then tried to persuade his people to follow his example, telling them that his creed was better than theirs. To this they replied: 'Let us subject ourselves to the ordeal of fire.' The king consented and a great fire was lit. The first to approach the fire were the pagans, with their idols

No pictures of Dhu Nuwas remain, but this carving of one of his predecessors shows what such a portrait might have looked like (see also colour opp. p. 129)

The warships of Byzantium, Dhu Nuwas's powerful enemy

in their hands, but they could not bear the heat and retreated. Then the two Jewish sages approached the fire, with scrolls of the Torah wrapped around their necks, and the fire did them no harm. Thus the Himyarites were persuaded to convert to Judaism.

Joseph Dhu Nuwas succeeded to the throne in 517 or 518 CE. He was not the heir to the king who had preceded him, but nevertheless was of royal extraction. According to legend his predecessor was a lecherous man who, being in constant fear of being overthrown, used to invite young men of royal descent to his banquets, and to kill them there. One day young Dhu Nuwas received such an invitation. Suspecting treachery, he hid a sharp knife in his boots, and went to meet the king. When they were alone the king suddenly leapt towards Dhu Nuwas, trying to kill him, but Dhu Nuwas was quicker; after a short struggle he managed to kill the king. On the same day he was placed on the throne by the king's men, who were happy to be rid of the tyrant.

Dhu Nuwas proved to be a very good ruler. His first step was to unite the various tribes of Himyar under his supremacy. He then turned to making alliances with external powers, such as Parthia, in order to thwart the intrigues of Byzantium and the Ethiopians. He also maintained relations with the sages of the land of Israel, seeking their counsel and encouragement. Proof of relations of another kind between Israel and Himyar was unearthed in the famous necropolis of Beth She'arim in the valley of Jezreel, where the inscription 'Himyarites' was found in one of the burying-halls.

In 522 an Ethiopian army invaded Himyar, and, taking advantage of the absence of Dhu Nuwas and his army, captured the capital, Zafar, and other places in Himyar. Hearing this bad news, Dhu Nuwas hastened to the rescue of his capital. He first sent four envoys, two Jewish sages and two Christians, to try and persuade the besieged Ethiopians to surrender. Since they refused to do so he ferociously attacked the place and dealt the Ethiopians a crushing defeat, forcing them to retreat to their own country.

Since the Christian population of Himyar cooperated with the Ethiopians during their short occupation, Dhu Nuwas punished the Christian Himyarites severely for their treason. In some places churches were burned down and some Christians were killed. One of the Christians managed to escape on horseback across the desert and informed the Byzantine emperor of what had happened. Thereupon the emperor asked the king of Ethiopia, who was his vassal, to punish Dhu Nuwas.

In the spring of 525, 120,000 Ethiopian soldiers crossed the Red Sea in Byzantine ships and invaded Himyar. Dhu Nuwas faced danger from outside and treason from within, for some of the Himyarite tribes refused to rally around his banner. Nevertheless, Dhu Nuwas marched against the Ethiopians, disregarding their numerical superiority. A fierce battle ensued on the shores of the Red Sea. Dhu Nuwas and his men fought with all their might, but

OPPOSITE Joseph Trumpeldor as an officer in the Russian army

BELOW Czar Nicholas II, 'little father' of all Russians, blessing his troops

the Ethiopian army was much stronger. One after the other his generals and soldiers fell. At last, seeing that the battle was lost and abhorring the thought of falling into the hands of the Ethiopians, Dhu Nuwas spurred his noble horse and sprang off the cliffs into the depths of the Red Sea.

Joseph Trumpeldor

Joseph Trumpeldor was born in 1880 at Piatigorsk in the Russian Caucasus. His father was a veteran of the army of Czar Nicholas I, in which he served for twenty-five years. His family lived outside the mainstream of Jewish life, but Joseph's father wanted him to be conscious of his Jewishness, and therefore sent the young boy to study in a Jewish *heder* for a couple of months. After attending an elementary municipal school Joseph wanted to continue his studies in a secondary school, but he was not admitted because he was a Jew.

Not being able to study properly, Trumpeldor asked his elder brother, who was a dentist, to teach him his profession. When he was twenty-two, Trumpeldor received the diploma of a dental practitioner, after taking the proper examinations in the University of Kazan. Shortly afterwards he was called for military service. Having an academic degree, he could have trained as an officer, but he refused to do so, and volunteered as a private. 'I want first to distinguish myself on the battlefield,' he told his astounded friends. Life as a private soldier in the army of the czar was harsh,

ABOVE A group of comrades training in Eastern Europe before they went out to found Kibbutzim (communal farms)

CENTRE Tel Hai, lonely and endangered settlement in Upper Galilee

OPPOSITE Crowds gathered in the rain in 1934 when the monument to Trumpeldor was unveiled at Tel Hai

but Trumpeldor, who was physically strong, bore it with ease, and won the esteem of his commanders. In 1904 war broke out between Russia and Japan. Trumpeldor was very anxious to be sent to the front, but to his surprise found that he was to be sent to an officers' school. He thereupon asked for an interview with the general of his division and insisted that he should go to the front. At last his wish was granted and he was dispatched to Port Arthur. There he distinguished himself to the utmost. On one occasion he managed to save the life of his comrades by quickly throwing back a Japanese hand grenade. Another time he led a surprise attack, inspiring his comrades with his personal bravery. Then on 6 August 1904, during a fierce clash with the enemy, Trumpeldor's left arm was severely injured. At the hospital the doctor decided that the arm must be amputated, and he submitted to the operation without anaesthetics.

Trumpeldor spent more than three months in hospital. When he was well again he was summoned for an interview with the commander of his regiment. The colonel presented him with a medal for bravery, saying that he should now return home and enjoy his rights as an invalid. Trumpeldor proudly answered: 'I have only one hand, but it is the right one. I want to return to my comrades and fight again. I therefore request your Excellency to arrange that I am given a sword and a pistol.' His request was granted, his courage commended, and he was made the commander of a platoon. Unlike other Russian officers, he actually led his men into battle.

A month later the Russian forces in Port Arthur surrendered and the Russian soldiers (Trumpeldor among them) were taken to a prisoner-of-war camp in Japan. There he showed his rare talent as an organizer. He founded a federation of Jewish Prisoners, an elementary school for all prisoners, a mutual aid fund, a Jewish theatre, and a Jewish weekly. He also organized a Zionist circle with over 150 members. In 1906 he was released from captivity

and went back to Russia. He was presented to the Russian royal family, was promoted and received a gold medal. At that time Trumpeldor was the highest ranking Jewish officer in the Russian army. A handsome man, he found favour in the eyes of the Russian Princess Gagarina, who offered him a brilliant military career if only he would consent to be converted to Christianity. He refused, and entered the faculty of law in St Petersburg University.

At university he decided that after completing his studies he would go to the land of Israel along with a group of his friends and establish a communal agricultural settlement, even learning to plough with his only hand. Arriving in the country in 1912, he and his friends established their commune near Lake Galilee, but it failed, and the commune dispersed. Trumpeldor then went to Deganyah, the first kibbutz in the land. There he took an active part in everything, working better with his one arm than some others did with both.

At the outbreak of World War I Trumpeldor was arrested as an alien by the Turkish authorities (who then ruled the country) and jailed in Damascus. After a while he was released and went to Alexandria in Egypt. There he was instrumental in founding a Jewish regiment, with the aim of helping the British forces to liberate the country from Turkish rule. The British authorities did not consent to these far-reaching plans. Instead they turned the Jewish regiment into a supply unit called the Zion Mule Corps and sent it to the Gallipoli front. The commanding officer of the Corps was an English colonel. Trumpeldor was his second-in-command, bearing the rank of captain. In Gallipoli as in Port Arthur, Trumpeldor's courage was outstanding. Seated upright on his horse, he scorned the flying bullets as he led his men. When the English commander of the Corps fell ill and was sent to Alexandria, Trumpeldor became commander of the Zion Mule Corps. At the beginning of 1916 the Corps was disbanded. Trumpeldor then went to London.

In the spring of 1917, a few months after the first revolution in Russia, Trumpeldor returned to Russia. He tried to interest the Provisional Government in his plan to establish a division of Russian Jews, numbering 100,000 soldiers, which would fight on the Caucasus front, and afterwards fight its way to the land of Israel. Meanwhile he organized a Jewish regiment to defend the Jewish population against possible pogroms by the 'White' forces. The Bolshevik revolution put an end to Trumpeldor's plans. He then turned to the organization of a Zionist movement, He-Halutz. Under the cover of spurious Communist organizations Trumpeldor established training farms in the Crimea.

In 1919 Trumpeldor was sent to the land of Israel on behalf of He-Halutz to study the conditions and the prospects for immigration. At that time the Turks had withdrawn, but no peace treaty had been signed. Britain and France, allies in the treaty, both claimed some form of authority over the territory. French troops held Lebanon and Upper Galilee. On arrival, he learned of the perilous situation of the four small Jewish settlements in Upper Galilee: Hamra, Tel Hai, Kefar Giladi and Metula, each one of which contained only a few score of settlers. In both Kefar Giladi and Tel Hai there were only forty-three men and four women. They had thirty-four guns, with only a hundred cartridges each. In 1919, during a local Arab uprising, the French forces had to evacuate Upper Galilee. The Arabs then started attacking the Jewish settlements, claiming that the Jews were helping the French. The situation was critical. The Arab forces numbered a couple of thousand, all well equipped, but the settlers were resolved to defend their homes and fields to the bitter end.

Trumpeldor decided that at such a critical hour he should be with the settlers, and at the end of December 1919 he hastened to Tel Hai and assumed command. The Arab attacks continued, but the settlers kept on working in their fields. Their ammunition was dwindling, their food supplies were waning, but still they held their ground. In February one of the defenders of Tel Hai was killed while working in the fields.

On 1 March 1920 Trumpeldor and some of the defenders of Tel Hai were in Kefar Giladi, when suddenly they heard shooting from the direction of Tel Hai. Rushing there, they found that the place was surrounded on three sides, but Trumpeldor and his men managed to get inside the fortified courtyard. Once inside they were surprised to find that the other defenders had let several Arab officers enter the place on the grounds that they wanted to make sure that no French soldiers were hiding in Tel Hai. The Arab officers searched everywhere until at last there was only one place left, the second floor of a house which served as a defence position for the settlers. Pretending that they wanted to check this place as well, the Arabs suddenly grabbed the pistol out of the hands of Deborah Drechler, one of the defenders.

OPPOSITE ABOVE Pharaoh's chariot in pursuit of Moses and the Jews, who had just been released from Egypt after the ten plagues

OPPOSITE BELOW Roman siege engine of a type used against Bar Kokhba's forces

Trumpeldor ran towards the open gate to try and block the advance of the Arabs waiting outside. After a couple of paces he was hit in his hand by a bullet, but he kept on running. A second bullet hit him in the stomach. He sagged to the ground in a critical state, though still conscious. After he had been dragged to a nearby hut, he passed the command to Pinhas Shneurson.

The fight lasted for eight hours. When night came five of the defenders of Tel Hai were dead (including Deborah Drechler), but they were still holding the Arabs back. Under the cover of darkness reinforcement, including a doctor, arrived from Kefar Giladi. Finally it was decided to evacuate Tel Hai. The defenders left the settlement at midnight, carrying their wounded and dead, after setting their buildings on fire so that nothing could fall into the hands of the attackers. Trumpeldor was carried on a stretcher. As the sombre procession neared Kefar Giladi, Trumpeldor died. He was buried alongside his dead comrades in a grave between Tel Hai and Kefar Giladi.

Trumpeldor's example encouraged the other Jewish settlers in Upper Galilee to remain. The fact that Upper Galilee became part of the State of Israel is due in no small measure to the courageous stand of Trumpeldor and his friends.

Mordecai Anielewicz

On 1 September 1939, the German army invaded Poland. Twenty-eight days later Warsaw surrendered to the Nazi conqueror. At that time about 380,000 Jews lived in Warsaw, and among them was a young man called Mordecai Anielewicz.

Twenty years earlier Mordecai was born into a working-class family and was brought up in one of the slums of Warsaw. The Polish boys in his neighbourhood often harassed the Jewish boys, and early in his short life Mordecai came to a decision which was to guide him throughout his life, until his death in the bunker in 18 Mila Street: never to submit – always to fight back. When Mordecai was fifteen he joined the Zionist-socialist pioneering youth movement, Ha-Shomer ha-Tza'ir. He soon rose in the movement, and by the time the Nazi army invaded Poland he was one of the leaders of the Warsaw branch.

A short time before Warsaw surrendered to the Germans, Mordecai, with some other members of his movement, decided to leave Warsaw and try to steal across the Rumanian border in order to reach Eretz Israel. Mordecai was caught at the border by a Russian patrol, but was released shortly afterwards. He returned to Warsaw, now under German control, to find the Jews of Warsaw being savagely persecuted: kidnapped in the streets for forced labour; physically and mentally humiliated; murdered. The whole Jewish population was in the shadow of imminent doom.

An identity photograph of the young Mordecai Anielewicz

After a few days in Warsaw Mordecai took to the road again. This time he went to Vilna, then still beyond the cruel clutch of the Nazis, where many members of the Zionist youth movements had found refuge. But Mordecai did not seek refuge. He could not forget Warsaw, and the boys and girls of his movement he had left there. He vehemently urged the executive of Ha-Shomer ha-Tza'ir to send people to Warsaw and to other parts of the area occupied by the Germans, to reorganize the movement clandestinely. Mordecai was among the first to return to Warsaw in the winter of 1939/40. With him went Mira, the girl he loved, who remained by his side, taking an active part in all that Mordecai did, until the last stand on 8 May 1943.

On the Day of Atonement 5701 (12 October 1940), the Nazis ordered the establishment of a ghetto in Warsaw. Within a month all the Jews of Warsaw (including Jewish refugees from the provinces) had to move to an assigned area, while its Polish inhabitants had to evacuate it. In April 1941 there were 445,000 Jews living in the ghetto, in area comprising only eight per cent of the total area of Warsaw although its inhabitants comprised forty per cent of the total population of the city. The average number of persons per room was thirteen, not to speak of the thousands who remained homeless in the severe Polish winter. The ghetto was surrounded by a wall ten feet high and twelve miles long, which the Jews themselves were forced to build.

Conditions in the ghetto were horrible. It was the last stage on the long journey to the death camps, its aim being to concentrate the Jewish population, to cut it off from the outside world, to ruin any social organization, with the people living in constant uncertainty or even terror. Above all, the ghetto was intended to break the spirit, vitality and resistance of the Jews by subjecting them to life at its hardest and humiliating, so that hunger, epidemics (especially typhoid) and the hardships of the weather might increase their mortality and make the Final Solution an easier task for the Germans. The ghetto population received a food allocation amounting to 184 calories per person a day (as compared with the 2,310 allocated to a German). Small wonder that every morning scores of dead were found in the streets. By the summer of 1942, over 100,000 Jews had died.

Mordecai and his friends had to cope with these conditions. First they tended the body by organizing an urban commune and a free kitchen for the members of the movement. Then they tended the soul by organizing educational activities and publishing an underground paper ('Against the Stream'). Mordecai was instrumental in all those activities. By the beginning of 1942 rumours of massacres in the Vilna ghetto (then under Nazi control), and extermination by gas in other places began to seep into the Warsaw ghetto. The leaders of the Jewish political underground began to grasp the full extent of the Nazi scheme: total annihilation of the Jewish people. All energies were now devoted to the formation of an armed underground, which would be able to attack the Germans and delay them, the moment they began to liquidate the ghetto. But the crucial problem was how to acquire arms: guns, ammunition, hand grenades and explosives. The only possible source of arms at that time was the right wing of the Polish underground, but it was heavily anti-Semitic and would not cooperate with the Jews.

In May 1942 Mordecai slipped out of the ghetto and went to western Poland to organize underground Jewish resistance. Shortly afterwards the Germans began to break up the Warsaw ghetto by transporting large numbers of its inhabitants to gas chambers in the death camp of Treblinka. The transport orders were preceded by a massacre intended to intimidate the inhabitants. The Jewish underground was not prepared for this crisis; it had no arms at all! And thus the Germans were able to carry out their plan almost without any obstacle. By employing brutal force and murder on one hand, and by luring the starving Jews with promises of 'bread and jam' on the other hand, the Germans were able to deport an average of 6,000 Jews a day. In fifty days the Germans murdered and transported to Treblinka 300,000 Jews. Only 70,000 were left in the ghetto, half of them 'illegally'.

The moment this terrible news reached Mordecai he returned to the ghetto. In October 1942 an underground Jewish Fighting Organization (JFO) was created in the ghetto and Mordecai was named its commander. Why was such a young man, not yet

A boy in the Vilna ghetto before the Nazi occupation

ABOVE Boarding the train to death: destination Treblinka

OPPOSITE Life in the ghetto was rigorously controlled by means of ration cards and work permits. These were ways of making it impossible for the Jews to escape from the ghetto and of keeping them physically weak

twenty-four years old, elected to such an important position? Says a man who knew Mordecai in the ghetto: 'Mordecai was energetic, he was a self-contained man and self-reliant. He was a man who devoted all his energy to one cause, and this cause was Jewish armed resistance, Jewish vengeance.' The aim of the JFO was to resist any further deportation. It now was somewhat easier to obtain arms from the Polish underground and about a hundred pistols and some hand grenades were smuggled into the ghetto. In the ghetto itself secret workshops manufactured self-made hand grenades and bombs. A system of subterranean bunkers was built, especially for the non-fighting members of the population. Since the houses of the ghetto were built with their walls at a tangent, the fighters bored holes into the walls, so that when the fighting started they would be able to pass from one house to another without being spotted by the enemy. At the same time the JFO decided to clear from the ghetto all the Jewish collaborators with the Nazis. The JFO sentenced several such people to death and they were shot.

In January 1943 the following proclamation was published:

On 22 January, it shall be six months since the mass deportation of the Jews of Warsaw began. We all remember well the days of horror in which 300,000 of our brethren were taken away and slaughtered in the death camp of Treblinka. Since then six months have elapsed, six months in which we have lived in a perpetual fear of death, without knowing what tomorrow might bring. From all around we receive information on the extermination of the Jews. Day after day, hour after hour we are waiting for our inevitable hour to come . . . Jew! That hour is approaching. You *must* be ready to defend yourselves! Do not stretch your necks to the hangman! No Jew will go to the death-train! Those who cannot fight, must fight in a passive way by hiding from the Nazis . . . Our motto *must* be: we shall die as men.

A child's drawing of Mordecai Anielewicz leading the ghetto revolt

Children in Lodz, another Polish ghetto

But the Germans did not wait till 22 January. Four days earlier, on 18 January 1943, the ghetto was surrounded, and a second mass deportation began, with the intention of transporting 16,000 Jews to Treblinka. But this time it was different. Although the JFO was still ill-equipped, Mordecai decided that the time had come. He was cool-headed and decisive in giving his orders, and the fighters who had waited so long for that moment to come were more than willing to obey him. As the Germans herded groups of Jews towards the railway station, Mordecai headed a group of ten fighters, who mingled among the walking Jews. They had five pistols and five hand grenades. Each fighter chose 'his' German soldier. Then, as they were approaching the railway station the sign was given. Margalith Landau, an eighteen-year-old girl, threw a hand grenade at the Germans. The fighters started shooting. Mordecai, whose pistol was jammed, leapt barehanded for one of the German soldiers and wrenched the gun out of his hands. But soon the Germans reorganized their forces and fired back. Mordecai was the sole survivor. Other groups of the JFO attacked German soldiers who tried to enter the houses which they were holding. The Germans did not dare to enter the houses and they were cautious in the streets as well.

German troops dragging Jews out of their hiding places among the rubble

After four days of fighting the Germans decided to stop the deportations, afraid that the example of the fighting ghetto would spread to other places in Poland. But Mordecai and the Jewish fighters knew that the Germans could come again, and therefore prepared for the final stand. The Germans did come. The final extermination of the ghetto was fixed for the eve of Passover, 19 April 1943. A large German force with tanks and artillery entered the ghetto. The Jewish fighters watched it from their hidden positions. As the Germans approached, Mordecai gave the order. Heavy fire was opened on the Nazis. After some hours of fighting, the unbelievable happened. Despite their overwhelmingly superior forces, the Germans had to retreat from the ghetto, leaving many casualties behind them. The commander of the German force was relieved from his post, and replaced by an S.S. general. The attack on the ghetto was resumed at once; but Mordecai and his men fought with superior courage and the Germans had very little success, suffering many casualties.

After several days of hard fighting the Germans changed their tactics. They avoided open clashes with the Jews. Instead they started burning down one block of houses after the other, thus depriving the Jewish fighters of their hiding places. The Germans also employed special equipment for discovering the hidden bunkers, and when they discovered one, they used large quantities of explosives to burst it open. Even then the inhabitants of the bunker would not come out of their free will. They shot at the Germans until they ran out of ammunition. In order to force the Jews out of the bunkers the Germans used gas. Nevertheless, the ghetto still resisted with desperate courage. Here is what Mordecai wrote in his last letter, which was smuggled from the ghetto: 'I cannot describe the horrible circumstances in which the Jews are living. Only few will survive; all the others will die, sooner or later. Our fate is sealed. In all the bunkers in which our men are hiding, it is impossible to light a candle at night, because of the lack of fresh air . . . Farewell my friend! Maybe we shall meet some day. But the important thing is that the dream of my life has become true: I have lived to see a mighty Jewish resistance in the Ghetto!'

In spite of the intolerable conditions in which they lived, Jewish groups continued to attack the Germans, especially in night raids. On 8 May the end came: the Germans discovered the bunker at 18 Mila Street, the headquarters of the Jewish Fighting Organization. Mordecai and some hundred and twenty fighters were defending it. In the ensuing battle, Mordecai and over a hundred of his men were killed.

Thus fell Mordecai Anielewicz, the twenty-four-year-old commander of the Warsaw ghetto uprising, realizing in his death the dream of his life: to die fighting.

GIDEON FUKS

The heroism of the Warsaw ghetto fighters is still remembered throughout the world, as shown in this picture taken in New York in 1966

Drudgery

Rabbi Levi Yitzhak* discovered that the girls who knead the dough for the unleavened bread drudged from early morning until late at night. Then he cried aloud to the congregation gathered in the House of Prayer: 'Those who hate Israel accuse us of baking the unleavened bread with the blood of Christians. But no, we bake them with the blood of Jews!'

MARTIN BUBER

*Rabbi Levi Yitzhak of Berditchev was a hasidic *zaddik*, or teacher. For more about the Hasidim, see p. 76–81

The Martyrs

Jewish suffering, when it was unavoidable, was not seen as merely passive. Though it was not permitted to deny one's religion to save one's life, some Jews, especially in Christian Spain and in other countries, did submit to force and adopt Christianity or Islam. Many continued to practise Judaism in secret, a fact which cost them their lives if it became known. Others, however, spurned this escape, preferring to die proudly for the glory of the Name of God. Martyrdom of this positive kind was a great source of inspiration to the Jews in troubled times, and the roll of martyrs' names had an honoured place in the synagogue. This concept of death as a witness to God died when Jews were rejected no longer on religious grounds but as an inferior race. Of the millions murdered by the Nazis, many showed great courage, but few were able to regard their deaths as martyrdom.

And it came to pass after these things, that God did prove Abraham, and said unto him: 'Abraham,' and he said: 'Here am I.' And He said: 'Take now thy son, thine only son, whom thou lovest, take Isaac, and get thee into the land of Moriah, and offer him there for a burnt-offering upon one of the mountains which I will tell thee of.' And Abraham rose early in the morning, and saddled his ass, and took two of his young men with him, and Isaac his son, and he cleaved the wood for the burnt-offering and rose up, and went unto the place of which God had told him. On the third day Abraham lifted up his eyes and saw the place afar off. And Abraham said unto his young men: 'Abide ye here with the ass, and I and the lad will go yonder, and we will worship, and come back to you.' And Abraham took the wood of the burnt-offering, and laid it upon Isaac his son, and he took in his hand the fire and the knife, and they went both of them together. And Isaac spoke unto Abraham his father, and said: 'My father.' And he said: 'Here am I, my son.' And he said: 'Behold the fire and the wood, but where is the lamb for the burnt-offering?' And Abraham said: 'God will provide himself the lamb for a burnt-offering, my son.' So they went both of them together. And they came to the place which God had told him of, and Abraham built the altar there and laid the wood in order, and bound Isaac his son, and laid him on the altar, upon the wood. And Abraham stretched forth his hand, and took the knife to slay his son.

The end of the story is too well known to need repeating here: God stopped Abraham's hand and provided him with a ram instead. He blessed Abraham for not withholding his son, saying 'I will multiply thy seed as the stars of the heavens and as the sand which is upon the seashore . . . and in thy seed shall all the nations of the earth be blessed, because thou hast hearkened to My Voice.'

This story, traditionally known as the *Akedah*, the 'binding' of Isaac to the altar to be sacrificed, has become in Jewish thought the supreme example of self-sacrifice in obedience to God's will and of readiness for martyrdom. When, in later ages, Jews were put

OPPOSITE The angel stops Abraham just as he is about to sacrifice Isaac at God's command (see also colour opp. p. 152)

to the supreme test they frequently fortified themselves with thoughts of the *Akedah*. Abraham's willingness to obey God sprang not from force or custom, honour or fear, but solely from the love of God, a love so strong and trusting that he offered his only son, for whose promised coming he had waited for decades, and in whose continued life alone could God's promise to Abraham be fulfilled. Such perfect faith and trust in God was what was needed in the trials and tribulations of the coming four thousand years of Jewish history. Jews who emulated Abraham's deed, most often by offering their own lives, performed their acts of sacrifice or self-sacrifice *Kiddush ha-Shem*, 'for the sanctification of the [Divine] Name'.

The term *Kiddush ha-Shem* is first found in Leviticus 22, verses 31–2: 'Ye shall keep My commandments and do them: I am the Lord. Ye shall not profane My holy Name, but I will be hallowed among the children of Israel, I am the Lord who hallows you.' The Lord hallows Israel by performing miracles for His people before the eyes of the world and by finally redeeming them. Jews hallow the Lord by living according to his commandments, avoiding evil and doing good. This was the original meaning of the term. Gradually, however, it came to be applied not to everyday behaviour but to special deeds performed under duress and while withstanding temptation. From this general moral sense *Kiddush ha-Shem* gradually evolved a special meaning which eventually overshadowed its original usage. It grew to indicate the deed which sanctified the Lord's name more than any other and was carried out under extreme duress – namely martyrdom.

The classical and more frequently quoted case of *Kiddush*

King Antiochus orders his servants to kill Hannah's seven sons for their refusal to eat pork

The Maccabean revolt. This illustration comes from a 16th-century edition of the works of Josephus, a Jewish historian who lived in the first century CE

ha-Shem is the story of the martyrdom of Hannah and her seven sons, as told in the second book of Maccabees:

Seven brothers with their mother had been arrested and were being tortured by the king with whips and tongs to force them to eat pork, when one of them, speaking for all, said: 'What do you expect to learn by interrogating us? We are ready to die rather than break the laws of our fathers.' The king was enraged and ordered great pans and cauldrons to be heated up, and this was done at once. Then he gave orders that the spokesman's tongue should be cut out and that he should be scalped and mutilated before the eyes of his mother and his six brothers.

One after the other the king, Antiochus Epiphanes, the ruler of Syria, had the brothers executed as they refused to defile themselves by eating unclean meat.

The mother was the most remarkable of all, and deserves to be remembered with special honour. She watched her seven sons all die in the space of a single day, yet she bore it bravely because she put her trust in the Lord, encouraging her sons with the words:

it was not I who gave you life and breath and set in order your bodily frames. It is the Creator of the universe who moulds man at his birth and plans the origin of all things. Therefore he, in his mercy, will give you back life and breath again, since now you put his laws above all thoughts of self.

The significance of their sacrifice, and the reason why they believed it to be vital, can best be explained in the story of Eleazar, a a ninety-year-old scribe, subjected to the same threat during the Maccabean revolt. Because they had known him for many years, the officials in charge of this sacrilegious feast had a word with Eleazar in private; they urged him to bring meat which he was permitted to eat, and only pretend to be eating the sacrificial meat as the king had ordered. Eleazar refused, as he sensed that not only he personally was being put to the test, but that the king intended, through him, to abuse and wipe out Judaism itself. If his life only had been at stake, saving it would have been his primary obligation, towards himself, his family, people and religion, all of which exist to be lived for. Antiochus, however, wished to force people to abjure their religion publicly and accept another – and therefore Eleazar was forced to prove, by his supreme sacrifice, that he preferred dying as a Jew to becoming an idolator, that the God and people of Israel live on because they are worth dying for.

The revolt of the Maccabees ended in a Jewish victory. The Jews' faith in their God had been vindicated in the attainment of independence. The memory of these deeds lived on and became a part of the heritage of the people, one which provided a forceful example in times of crisis. The victory of the Maccabees brought about the creation of the independent kingdom of Judaea, which soon, however, fell under the yoke of the Romans. Though the Romans were much more tolerant at first than the rulers of Syria,

King Antichous, on a coin issued during his reign

OVERLEAF Masada, the fortress above the Dead Sea (see also colour opp. p. 153)

141

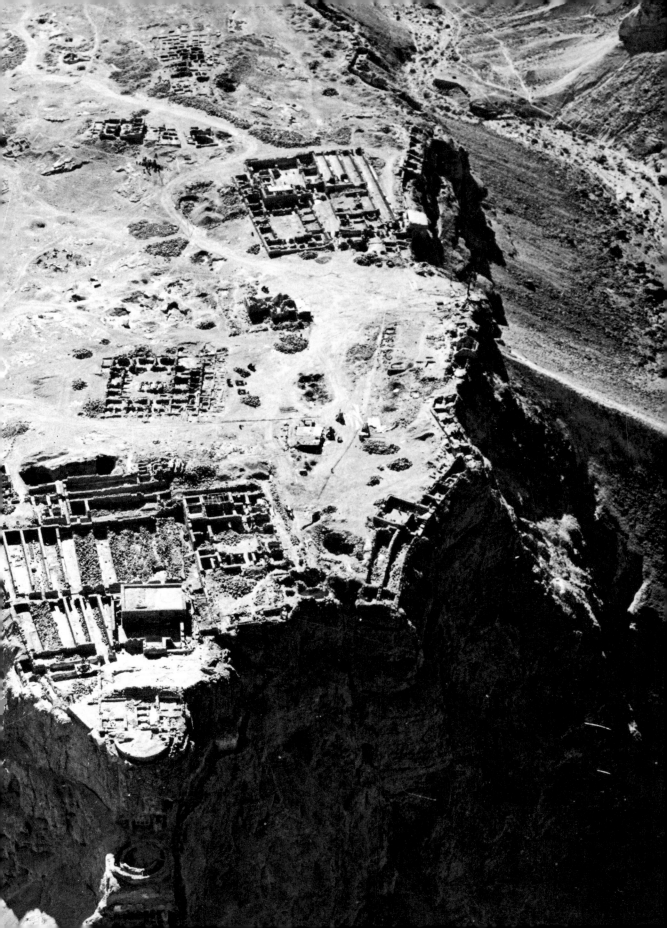

points of friction repeatedly arose between the secular-minded rulers and their religious-centred subjects. The willingness of the Jews to emulate the deeds of Hannah and Eleazar was narrowly averted a number of times. Thus they prepared themselves for *Kiddush ha-Shem* when the Romans intended to force their standards bearing the imperial image into the Holy City of Jerusalem, during the governorship of Pontius Pilate in 36/37 CE.

Thirty years later, in 66 CE, the mutual misunderstanding and distrust could no longer be contained, and a desperate rebellion broke out against Roman misrule in the province of Judaea. National, social and religious causes brought about a violent upsurge of feeling against Rome; the same causes undermined continued unified action against the common enemy and the rebellion petered out into a vicious civil war over ends and means. The most radical group of all were the Sicarii, the dagger bearers, who were spearhead and vanguard of the war-party (also known as the Zealots). Driven to desperation at the approach of total defeat, in 70 CE 960 men, women and children of the Zealot party fought their way through superior Roman forces till they found refuge in Masada, Herod's royal stronghold near Ein Gedi, high above the Dead Sea, in the Judaean desert, which was a natural and almost impregnable fortress.

The Romans did not attempt to attack it until the rebellion had been completely put down. Then they assembled their vastly superior forces and laid siege to it, knowing that there was no chance of starving the defenders into surrender. They built a solid platform 300 feet high, and on top of it a pier composed of great stones fitted together, 75 feet in width and height. On this, they constructed a great battering ram, which was swung continuously against the wall till at long last a breach was made and a small section collapsed. Inside, however, the defenders had lost no time in building a second wall, partially made of wood, which absorbed the blows of the ram. The legionaries flung a volley of burning torches against this wall and it caught fire. Just as the fire broke out a gust of wind blew back the flames and it seemed as if the Roman engines might be consumed. Then all of a sudden, the wind reversed and turned the wall into one blazing mass.

All hope was lost. The leader of the defenders, Eleazar ben Yair, collected the hardiest of his comrades and spoke to them:

My loyal followers, long ago we resolved to serve neither the Romans nor anyone else but only God, who alone is the true and righteous Lord of men. Now the time has come that bids us prove our determination by our deeds. At such a time we must not disgrace ourselves: hitherto we have never submitted to slavery, even when it brought no danger with it: we must not choose slavery now, and with it penalties that will mean the end of everything if we fall alive into the hands of the Romans. For we were the first of all to revolt, and shall be the last to break off the struggle, and I think it is God who has given us this privilege, that we can die nobly and as free men, unlike

OPPOSITE From the Middle Ages right up to the early 20th century, Jews were persecuted because they were accused of horrible practices, usually supposed to be perversions of Christianity. One such belief, that they crucified a Christian child and used his blood to make unleavened bread for Passover (in mockery of Easter) is ironically referred to in the story, 'Drudgery', on p. 137. This picture, a kind of early strip cartoon, shows another common twisted notion. A Jewish woman buys the kind of wafer biscuit (the Host) used in the Mass. When she and her family torture the Host, symbolizing the body of Jesus, blood flows from the wafer out of the door, which shocked soldiers batter down. These obviously silly stories were widely believed and made the excuse for tormenting and harassing Jews

others who were unexpectedly defeated. In our case it is evident that day-break will end our resistance, but we are free to choose an honourable death with our loved ones. This our enemies cannot prevent, however earnestly they may pray to take us alive; nor can we defeat them in battle ... Let our wives die unabused, our children without knowledge of slavery: after that, let us do to each other an ungrudging kindness, preserving our freedom as a glorious shroud.

Let us die unenslaved by our enemies, and leave this world as free men in company with our wives and children. That is what the Law ordains, that is what our wives and children demand of us, the necessity God has laid on us, the opposite of what the Romans wish – they are anxious none of us should die before the town is captured. So let us deny the enemy their hoped-for pleasure at our expense, and without more ado leave them dumbfounded by our death and awed by our courage.

His hearers rushed off, each to his own family, and clinging resolutely to the purpose they had formed while listening to Eleazar's appeal, they embraced their loved ones for the last time before ending their lives. The men chose ten by lot to be the executioners of the rest of them. Every man lay down beside his dead wife and children and exposed his throat. The remaining ten, after fulfilling their duty, were pierced by the sword of the one chosen by lot, who then fell on his own sword.

After the war peace reigned for two generations, but the outbreak of the rebellion of Bar Kokhba in 132 CE, during Emperor Hadrian's rule, proved that the tradition of heroic self-sacrifice in battle had not been forgotten (see pp. 116–22). The recurring rebellions in the province of Judaea angered and exasperated the Romans, who came to suspect that the obstinate refusal of the Jews to accept their yoke meekly was somehow connected with their peculiar religion. After protracted sieges and much bloodshed the country was pacified, and in order to punish the Jews and to eradicate the sources of their stubborn recalcitrance the Romans prohibited the study and teaching of the Torah. This decree, if carried through, would have sounded the death-knell of Judaism, and Jewish spiritual leaders arose who defied it at the price of their lives. Ten of them were remembered by posterity by being the subject of the Day of Atonement prayer known as *Eleh Ezkerah*.

The most famous of the Ten Martyrs was Rabbi Akiva, the greatest sage of his generation, who had decisive influence on the formation of Judaism after the destruction of the Temple.

It occurred that when Rabbi Akiva was being executed the time for the *Shema* benediction recitation arrived; while they were lacerating his flesh with iron combs he was preparing himself to carry out the will of the Kingdom of Heaven devotedly. His pupils asked: 'Our Teacher, Even so far?' He replied: 'All my life I have regretted not being able to carry out the commandment, "to love the Lord with all my soul" – even though he takes it away. And now that the occasion has arrived ought I to avoid fulfilling it?' While prolonging the recitation of the *Shema* his soul departed. When the news that Rabbi Akiva had been executed in Caesarea reached Rabbi Judah

OPPOSITE The Synagogue at Hódmezövásárhely, Hungary

ben Baba and Rabbi Hanina ben Tardion they put on sackcloth in mourning and said: 'Listen, our brethren, Children of Israel: Rabbi Akiva did not die for a crime committed or for not studying the Torah with all his might, but in order to set an example.'

Rabbi Akiva's example in reciting this most central prayer at the decisive moment was followed by succeeding generations during their own trial of faith.

With the loss of independence and the gradual decline of the population, the land of Israel ceased to be the main centre of Jewish life. Large communities were established in other countries. In the early Middle Ages, the Jews of Babylon, at first the most important community, gradually lost their pre-eminence to the new Jewry which had arisen in the West. In northern France and the Rhineland new and prosperous communities developed, small islands of Judaism in an increasingly intolerant and hostile Christian environment. These small Ashkenazi communities (differentiated from the Sephardi ones of the East) were proud of their peculiar position and individual tradition of liturgy and scholarship.

After many decades of tranquil existence they were plunged into a cataclysm of bloodshed and despair by the events which accompanied the Crusades. During the First Crusade (1096 CE), persecutions of the Jews took place which differed from those of the ancient world, and became characteristic of those of the medieval era. The persecutions and massacres were very widely distributed and encompassed almost all Christian Europe; Jews were massacred in the places where the crusaders were assembled along their route to the Holy Land. The many current religious, social and economic problems, which were in fact a result of the type of society then in force, were laid at the door of the Jews. Religious fanaticism, intolerance and the superstition of the masses became allied

Roman missile launching pad of the type used against the Zealots

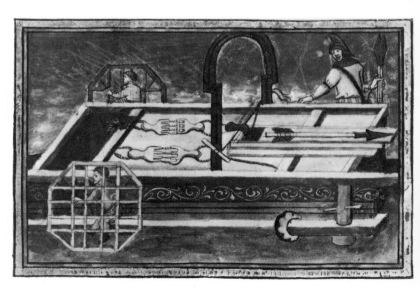

A *bar mitzvah* at Masada, a continuing commemoration of the Zealots' courage

with their greed for easy plunder. Persecutions were particularly vicious and bloodthirsty, on a scale hitherto unknown; no quarter was given. The killing of Jews, the supposed infidel enemies of Jesus, became a religious obligation, and their only salvation lay in renouncing their religion. To this, the Jews responded by performing *Kiddush ha-Shem* on a scale and in a manner hitherto unknown.

On 27 May 1096, Emicho, a German nobleman, leading an army of 12,000 crusaders, forced his way into the Rhineland city of Mayence and finally into the palace of the archbishop, where the Jews had found refuge:

When the children of the holy covenant saw that the heavenly decree of death had been issued and that the enemy had conquered them and had entered the courtyard, then all of them – old men and young, maidens and children, servants and maids – cried out together to their Father in heaven, weeping for themselves and for their lives, accepted as just the judgement of God. They said to each other: 'Let us be strong and let us bear the yoke of the holy religion, for only in this world can the enemy kill us, and the easiest of deaths is by the sword. Our souls in paradise shall continue to live eternally, in the great shining reflection of divine glory' . . .

Then all of them, to a man, cried out with a loud voice: 'Now we must delay no longer for the enemy are already upon us. Let us hasten and offer ourselves as a sacrifice to the Lord. Let him who has a knife examine it that it be ritually fit, and let him come and slaughter us for the sanctification of the Only One, the Everlasting, and then let him cut his own throat or plunge the knife into his own body . . . The women there then girded their loins with strength and slew their daughters and then themselves. Many men, too, plucked up courage and killed their wives, their sons, their infants . . .

These terrifying events were repeated in dozens of communities where the Jews were faced with the choice of accepting baptism or being killed. *Kiddush ha-Shem* became the order of the day in fulfilment of the basic tenet of Judaism to worship no graven images and to commit no idolatry, as Catholicism was believed to do. The commandment to avoid idolatry at any cost created tragic and insoluble dilemmas for parents of young children who were sometimes kidnapped so that they could be brought up as pious Christians. Some Jewish parents, rather than have their children seized, acted like Rachel, the daughter of Rabbi Isaac ben Asher, the wife of Rabbi Judah, who said to her friends: 'I have four children. Do not spare even them, lest the Christians come to take them alive and bring them up in their false religion. Through them, too, sanctify the name of the Holy God!'

The events during the First Crusade described above by contemporary witnesses repeated themselves with tragic regularity throughout medieval Jewish history. Every Crusade became a time of dread and reckoning for the Jews. Whenever a plague or epidemic broke out, as they often did in those insanitary days, the Jews were blamed and accused of poisoning the wells, of wishing to revenge themselves upon the Christians. During the Black Death epidemic of 1348–9 the massacres of Jews assumed genocidic proportions. The Jews were often accused of using the blood of a Christian child in preparing the unleavened bread of Passover, the *matzot*, and whole communities were wiped out. Often riots and outbursts against the Jews had no justification whatsoever and broke out spontaneously on the flimsiest excuses. Very few Jews accepted Christianity willingly in western Europe in the Middle Ages, and many of those who were forcibly baptized waited impatiently for the times of trouble to pass so that they could revert to the faith of their fathers at the earliest possible moment.

In Spain, where the Jews had lived in prosperity and comparative peace under Arab rule, violent anti-Jewish riots swept the land in the fourteenth century. They were fanned by the preaching of Paul of Burgos, a fanatical Christian convert from Judaism. As the mobs poured into the Jewish communities, many of the inhabitants killed themselves rather than fall into the hands of their enemies, who offered life only in return for a change of religion. Many others accepted baptism rather than death. A century later these reluctant Christians were pursued by the Inquisition. For trying to live secretly as Jews, while being officially Christian, they were declared heretics and thus within the province of the Inquisition courts (which had nothing to do with Jews as such). Many of these secret Jews, who were called Conversos or Marranos, suffered a belated martyrdom for their determination to practise Judaism against all odds. Condemned to be burned at the stake, they reaffirmed the wavering faith of their grandfathers.

Kiddush ha-Shem was one expression of the struggle of Judaism

TOP An imaginary painting of Worms from the wall of a Russian synagogue. At Worms, too, the Jews were massacred during the First Crusade

ABOVE Jews being burned in a German market square after they had been accused of causing the Black Death through poisoning drinking wells

ABOVE Christian pilgrims marching on Jerusalem

LEFT ABOVE Peter the Hermit preaching during the First Crusade. When he demanded why they should travel so far to fight unbelievers, when unbelievers lived amongst them, the would-be Crusaders fell upon the Jews of the Rhineland.

LEFT BELOW In the Middle Ages Jews were frequently charged with hostile acts against Christians and Christianity. Here a Jew is shown stamping on a picture of the Virgin Mary at the command of the devil. Below, devils torture him to death. The belief that Jews were in league with the devil was very common.

in a hostile world. As Judaism was the weaker materially and politically it suffered agonies, while its stronger rival barely suffered pangs of conscience. Christian persecutors were motivated by many and various causes, one of which was a blind, misguided devotion to totally unchristian beliefs and superstitutions about the Jews. Fanaticism was mingled with faith and men's darker fears and horrors were fastened on the Jews.

The sentiments which had spearheaded anti-Jewish persecutions in the Middle Ages seemed however to wane and then to vanish in western Europe. Enlightened and optimistic Jews and Christians came sincerely to believe that the rule of reason and tolerance had arrived to stay and that the memory of persecution would slowly disappear, just as persecution itself was vanishing from the contemporary scene.

In czarist Russia, on the other hand, hatred of the Jews continued unabated. From the late nineteenth century especially, pogroms became government policy. The old medieval notion that the Jews were plotting to overthrow Christianity and gain control of the whole world was revived in 1903 in the *Protocols of the Elders of Zion*, a forged document which it was claimed revealed

The Holocaust

RIGHT An old woman in Auschwitz wearing the Jewish badge, a yellow Star of David

OPPOSITE ABOVE Dutch Jews being deported to Westerbok, and eventually to the death camps

OPPOSITE BELOW Belsen — emaciated victim and scarcely healthier survivors

BELOW Peasants in Sudetenland, who were of German origin though the area was in Czechoslovakia, greeting the arrival of the German army with Nazi salutes

the truth of the worldwide Jewish conspiracy. The last of the czars, Nicholas II, looked on unmoved while the Black Hundreds, a notorious anti-Jewish gang, swooped down on Jewish communities spreading havoc and death. Worst of the pogroms occurred in Kishinev in 1903.

Eight years later the medieval libel that Jews killed Christian children to use their blood for making *matzot* was also revived in Russia. The discovery of the mutilated body of a twelve-year-old boy outside the city of Kiev led to the arrest of Menachem Mendel on a charge of ritual murder. After two years in prison he was brought to trial and acquitted for lack of evidence, but the damage had been done. Old hatreds were revived afresh.

Meanwhile, the tide turned in western Europe also, and the prejudices of the modern secular and even anti-religious world surpassed in ferocity and thoroughness any bestiality of the past. The loss of faith in the modern world stripped the persecution of the last vestige of humanity: children were no longer spared in the hope of bringing them up as Christians and baptism was not even offered as salvation. All that remained was rage and hatred, often given a new 'scientific' basis with the growth of the pseudo-theory that the Jews were a genetically inferior race.

The continuing harassment of Jews and Judaism in czarist Russia was soon overshadowed by the events in the states of eastern Europe created after World War I (Poland, Hungary, Rumania) where millions of Jews were at the mercy of vicious anti-Semitic sentiments and movements. All over Europe the position of the Jews became precarious, dependent upon the stability of the economic and social situation. This stability was upset in the Depression which followed the American Wall Street crash of 1929. The Nazis came to power in Germany in 1933 and their imitators in most other European states within the next few years. The Nazis began carrying out Hitler's previously announced policy against the Jews, which no one had suspected was anything but the demonic outpourings of a warped mind. Nightmare had become reality, and within a few years, with the outbreak of World War II, the fate of the Jews in Europe became desperate. They were helpless, surrounded by the implacable hatred of their neighbours, a hatred nourished by the Nazi propaganda machine and fanned by repetition of all the ancient slanders against the Jews.

The murder of close to six million Jews by firing squads, in concentration camps, forced labour camps and extermination camps has raised a number of questions which have not been adequately answered to this day. How did it come about that the most cultured and civilized people in Europe behaved in the most barbaric manner possible? Why were there so very few cases of organized or unorganized Jewish resistance, the vast majority of the victims being led to slaughter uncomprehendingly or consciously resigning themselves to their fate? What, if any, is the historical significance of

OPPOSITE Abraham prepares to sacrifice Isaac

OVERLEAF Crusading soldiers (left) meet their Muslim adversaries on a bridge across the Danube.

rent en la tir de turquie
t la conquistrent en lan nre
seignor · m · cc · xl iiii ·

the Holocaust? Did it prove that God had forsaken His People? Was the Holocaust a supreme trial of faith, one which heralded the resurrection of the Jewish people in its ancestral homeland? Is there a line connecting the deeds of martyrs in the Middle Ages who sanctified the Divine Name and the six million martyrs of mankind's supreme inhumanity to man? A conclusive answer is of course impossible. It is clear that the victims' sole 'crime' was that they belonged to one particular people, and that the murderers' main intention was to eradicate Judaism and Jews from the face of the earth – thus making it the obligation of each and every Jew to vindicate his faith. Unlike in the medieval era the element of free choice was missing: the oppressor did not offer the victim the choice of conversion or death. Is death in a gas chamber at Auschwitz to be considered *Kiddush ha-Shem*? An affirmative answer would be comforting but would somehow detract from the deeds committed during the Crusades. The following story, told on the witness bench during the trial of Adolf Eichmann, one of the annihilators of European Jewry, illustrates some of the issues raised in the midst of the Holocaust.

Bauchwitz, of Stettin in Germany, was in charge of a group of Jews working outside the concentration camp. When one of them escaped he bore the responsibility himself and did not report the escape, for they used to kill ten men in the place of the one who escaped. When the escape was revealed they decided to hang him. He had one last request: 'I was a German officer in the First World War and I fought at the battle of Verdun. Of my whole battalion only a few survived and I received the Iron Cross citation, first class; as a former military man I request to be shot and not hanged.' The Nazis replied: 'For us you are a dirty Jew and will be hanged.' When Bauchwitz ascended the scaffold he requested the right to say a few words to the assembled Jews: 'I was born a Jew, but all I remember of my religion are a few words of one prayer . . . I die a Jew and request you Jews to say *Kaddish* for me.'

Bauchwitz was probably a highly educated person, one who had ignored his religion for decades and did not even remember the *Shema* at this most critical and appropriate moment. Yet his last wish was to die a Jew. The very determination of the Nazis to exterminate Judaism made the errant children of Israel aware of their religion. A revival of Judaism became a pronounced phenomenon under the most terrible conditions possible in the death camps. In the face of total degradation in the camps it became a question of life and death to retain one's own semblance of humanity – and the observance of Jewish ritual was just such a deed. The performance of the commandments became, under extreme conditions, a test of faith and of the will to live, and by living on to foil the oppressors' evil design.

HENRY WASSERMAN

A modern painter's vision of Babel riding with Budenny

Berestechko

Isaac Emmanuilovich Babel was born in the Russian port of Odessa in 1894. His mother tongue was Yiddish and his first efforts at writing were in French, yet he became one of the great masters of the Russian short story. The strangest episode in his life was when he, a poor-sighted intellectual Jew who admitted that he had no physical prowess and rode badly, fought for the Communist cause during the Russian revolution in a regiment of Cossacks. Not only were they traditional anti-Semites, but Babel had personal experience of their part in the 1905 pogroms, which he describes in *The story of my dovecote*. Although he had been a fighter for the Soviet regime, he was arrested by that regime in 1939. From that moment Babel disappeared, and it was later stated that he died in 1941. Many of his manuscripts were destroyed by the secret police.

The story printed here describes an event which took place during 1920 when Babel fought with Budenny's Cossack regiment in Poland. The Cossacks came not just to kill and plunder, but also to spread the doctrine of the brotherhood of man.

*   *   *

We were on the march from Khotin to Berestechko, and the men were dozing in their tall saddles. A song gurgled like a brook running dry. Grotesque corpses lay upon the age-old burial grounds. Peasants in white shirts doffed their caps to us. Divisional Commander Pavlichenko's felt cloak flew like a sombre flag above the staff. His downy Caucasian hood was thrown back over his cloak, and his curved sword hung down at his side.

We rode past the Cossack tumuli, past Bogdan Khmelnitsky's watchtower. From behind a burial stone an old fellow with a bandore crept forth and, plucking the strings, sang to us in a childish treble of the ancient glory of the Cossacks. We listened to his songs in silence; then unfurled the standards and burst into Berestechko to the sounds of a thundering march.

The inhabitants had put iron bars across their shutters, and silence, almighty silence, had ascended its small-town throne.

It so chanced that I was billeted in the house of a red-haired widow who smelt of the grief of widowhood. I washed away the traces of the march and went out into the street.

Notices were already posted up announcing that Divisional Commissar Vinogradov would lecture that evening on the second congress of the Comintern. Right under my window some Cossacks were trying to shoot an old silvery-bearded Jew for spying. The old man was uttering piercing screams and struggling to get away. Then Kudrya of the machine gun section took hold of his head and tucked it under his arm. The Jew stopped screaming and straddled his legs. Kudrya drew out his dagger with his right hand and carefully, without splashing himself, cut the old man's throat. Then he knocked at the closed window.

'Anyone who cares may come and fetch him,' he said. 'You're free to do so.'

Berestechko reeks unredeemably even now, and a violent smell of rotten herring emanates from all its inhabitants. The little town reeks on, awaiting a new era, and instead of human beings there go about the mere faded schemata of frontier misfortunes. I wearied of them by the end of the day, and leaving the town climbed a hill and penetrated into the sacked castle of the Counts Raciborski, late owners of Berestechko.

A meeting was being held in the square below. Peasants, Jews, and tanners from the outskirts had assembled there, with Vinogradov's voice above them, fired with enthusiasm, and the ringing of his spurs.

He talked about the second congress of the Comintern, while I wandered past walls where nymphs with gouged-out eyes were leading a choral dance.

Down below the Commissar's voice still goes on. He is passionately persuading the bewildered townsfolk and the plundered Jews.

'You are in power. Everything here is yours. No more *Pans* [Polish noblemen]. I now proceed to the election of the Revolutionary Committee . . .'

ISAAC BABEL translated by Walter Morison

Bogdan Khmelnitsky, leader of the revolt of the Ukraine against Polish rule. His irregular forces massacred the Jews of the Ukraine with such ferocity that most of the survivors fled. The greatest disaster to hit European Jewry since medieval times made many believe that the end of the world was near, a frame of mind that made them disposed to accept Shabbetai Zevi as the Messiah (see also p. 177)

The Dream of the Return

Dispersed as they were, the Jewish people never forgot that they had once had a homeland in Eretz Israel. In Sabbaths and holy festivals, the memory of the land, and of Jerusalem in particular, was kept alive. For some men 'next year in Jerusalem' represented more than a pious hope, and they set out on the long and perilous journey to the Holy Land. Some were captured and sold into slavery, some were robbed by bandits, some died on the way of sickness or shipwreck. Still some intrepid souls continued to make the attempt, defying the physical dangers and political prohibitions in force at the time. Scholars and mystics, merchants and explorers, all came, not in great numbers but with sufficient determination to keep alive the Jewish presence in the land.

I am very old and very young. Strong men weep when they first see me, and children's faces glow with delight when they touch me. Some sections of me are smooth, worn with the caresses of centuries; others are jagged and rough, untouched and unseen. I am silent and do not speak, but men come to me with their innermost thoughts. They share with me their hopes and dreams, their laughter and tears, their terrors and triumphs. They confide in me, they speak to me, and I listen. For two thousand years I have been listening and I have heard much and seen much and observed much.

Two thousand years. That is a long time. A people can wander the face of the earth in two thousand years, as my people have done. A people can suffer in two thousand years – and who has suffered more than the Jews? But in these two thousand years my people did not forget me. Others have been driven from lands and have forgotten their origins, but my people, wherever they were, remembered. In their homes they would hang drawings of me, tell stories about me, write poems to me. In their daily prayers they would pray to God to return to Zion, and they would plead: 'Return to Jerusalem Thy city in mercy, dwell in her as Thou hast spoken; rebuild her in our day, for eternity, and establish speedily the throne of David . . .' On the ninth day of the month Av, Jews in all corners of the Exile would dim their lights, remove their shoes, sit on the ground, and tearfully chant the mournful Book of Lamentations: 'how does she dwell alone, the city once filled with multitudes . . .' And the Jews would weep and fast through the night and day, as if they were mourning for the dead – because on the ninth of Av, the ancient Temple and city of Jerusalem were destroyed. I alone remained standing.

For I am the Wall. Only I am left from the ancient glory of King Solomon's Temple. I am known by many names: *ha-kotel ha-*

OPPOSITE The Western Wall in the 1930s

ma'aravi; the Western Wall; the Wailing Wall. Although not every Jew has seen me, every Jew knows me very well. For they never forgot me, or my city of Jerusalem, or my land, Eretz Israel. On all their festivals they prayed for me, and the Passover *seder* to this day ends with *Le-shana ha:ba'ah bi-Yerushalayim*, 'next year in Jerusalem'. And you surely know that the solemn Yom Kippur still ends with the same cry: 'Next year in Jerusalem.'

For some fortunate ones, next year did come. Despite the difficulties of travel, despite the hardships of the journey, and the weeks and months of trudging from the far corners of the earth, Jews constantly returned to me, and would go up the hills of Jerusalem and run towards me, fall to the earth and kiss me. They went on *aliyah* – which means *up* – up to the Land.

I am silent but I have seen much. The Crusaders who reached the Holy Land in the twelfth century wreaked havoc there too, as they had done in Europe (see pp. 146–8).

Those Jews who were fortunate escaped to the smaller towns in the countryside, and tried to eke out a bare living from the soil. Some grew sugar in the Jordan Valley, and others raised cotton in the Beisan Valley. Olive oil and soap were also very important products which helped some Jews make a living, while others worked as leather workers, blacksmiths, artisans, and traders in spices and medications. Some communities were so poor that they were forced to sell their most precious possession – the Sefer Torah – just in order to survive. But they did not leave the Land, for it was Eretz Israel, the land of their fathers.

Even though life in my country was difficult, my people around the world did not forsake me. For example, in the town of Cordova in twelfth-century Spain there lived a famous Jewish poet and philosopher, Judah Halevi (see pp. 101–3). He wrote hundreds of hymns and prayers to God, many of which became part of the Prayer Book and are still sung today in the synagogues. But his most beautiful songs and poems were about his love for Jerusalem, his longing for the holy soil. 'I am in the West,' he wrote, 'but my heart is in the East.' He expressed the spirit of the Jew in Exile, who is far away from his home and misses his familiar places. He knew that some day his people would be restored to their ancient homeland, and that all their wanderings and sufferings for God's sake would not have been in vain. He wrote that he would gladly part with all the wealth of Spain just to be able to glance for a brief moment at the last remnant of the ancient Temple which had been destroyed centuries before. If I only had the wings of a dove, he sang, I would immediately fly away just to breathe the fragrant air of Jerusalem.

After a number of years, Judah decided that it was not enough to write sad songs about the Land. He would go himself to Jerusalem. Although he had fame and fortune, he left it all behind and set sail in 1140. After a stormy voyage he came to Alexandria, in Egypt.

OPPOSITE Crusaders attacking Jerusalem, using the heads of their enemy as ammunition

desiroient si hautement enprendre leur
pruiner fer quetoutes les autres genz
les en doutassent.

Claire denique sachiez que le fu
soir leueschie deni come de. A ses len
pereres costentins la fist oster delpoir a cel

There were many Jews living in Egypt in those days and they wanted the famous Rabbi Judah to live among them. They offered him important positions of honour and glory, and promised him a life of ease and comfort. But Rabbi Judah knew that he must fulfil his life's goal. He wanted to set foot on the Holy Land, at least once, to see the site of the once-glorious Temple in Jerusalem. He wanted to have one glimpse of me, the Wall.

He left Egypt, came to the port city of Jaffa, and then to Jerusalem. Eagerly, he walked the narrow streets up the hill to the Temple Mount. His heart skipped as he approached me, and when he caught sight of the dust swirling out of the ruins of the destruction he wept tears of sadness mixed with joy. His poems, written in Spain, had now come true in Jerusalem, and they began to pour from him anew as he knelt in the dust at my feet.

But he did not arise from that dust. For as he lay there praying to God for the restoration of the Land, a horseman rode over him and killed him. Judah Halevi, the great poet of Jerusalem, lay now in the dust of the city which he loved more than anything else on earth.

About this time there were some three hundred Jewish families living in Jerusalem. There were Jews in smaller towns as well, such as Tiberias and Shechem. Some places had as few as two Jewish families. But no matter how small their numbers, my people clung stubbornly to the Land, and even the Crusaders with all their weapons and strength could not dislodge them.

This is one great quality of my people: they are stubborn and loyal. And wherever they lived, the Jews of the world continued to come back to me: the longing for the Land was overpowering. For example, in 1165, the father of the famous Maimonides left Spain with his family to come to Israel. He stayed a short time, visiting Acre, Jerusalem, and the graves of the patriarchs at Hebron; but conditions were so bad that he could not raise his growing family in the Land. So he went to the closest place, Egypt, hoping to return in a short while. Unfortunately, he died there. His oldest son, Moses ben Maimon – Maimonides – grew up to be the greatest Jewish leader of his time, known to all as *Rambam*, Rabbi Moshe ben Maimon (see pp. 97–101).

In 1160, another well-known Jew from Spain, Benjamin of Tudela, set out on a journey through Europe, Africa and Asia. And in 1169 he came to the Holy Land and visited Jerusalem. Benjamin was a great writer as well as a brave traveller, and his account of the journey is fascinating. His description of the Temple Mount and of conditions at that time is one of the few records available of what life was like in the twelfth century. Vividly he described the squalor and poor conditions of the Jews who clustered in little houses around the Temple area.

The Crusaders were not destined to stay very long in the country. In the year 1187, the Muslim general Saladin, governor of Egypt,

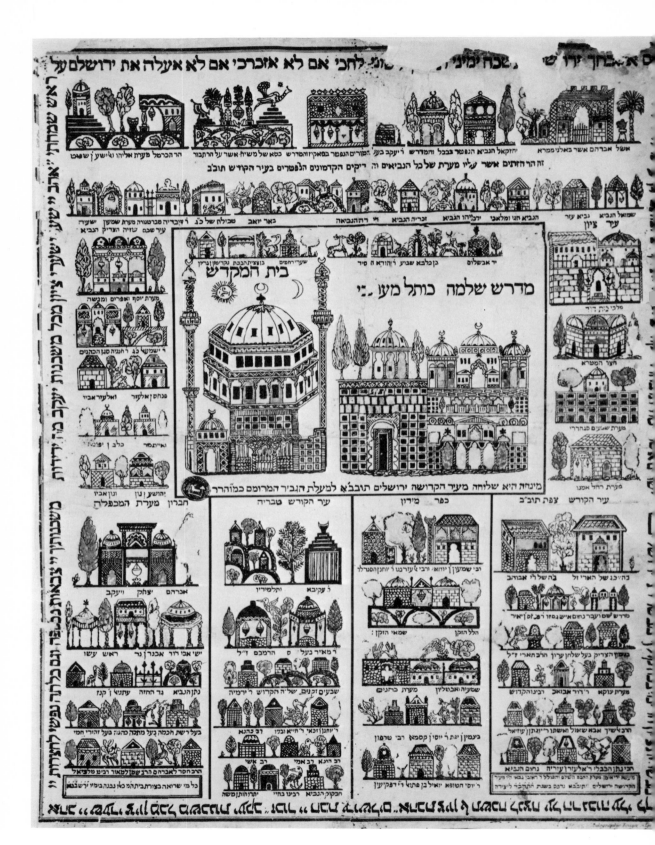

ΗΑΓΙΑΠΟΛΙΣΙΕΡΟΥСΑ ΚΛΗΡ

ΕΦΡΑΘΑ
ΡΑΜΑΦΩΝ
ΕΝΡΑΜ
ΗΚΟСΘ

ΒΗΘΛΕΕ ΡΜ

ΑΚΕΛ
ΔΑΜΑ

The oldest known map of Jerusalem, a mosaic from Madaba, Jordan, 6th century

OPPOSITE A diagram of the Jewish holy places in the land of Israel, showing Jerusalem in the centre and indicating the Western Wall

drove out the Crusaders and established his own dominion over Jerusalem. Saladin was a bit more tolerant of the Jews, and some who had fled to the countryside began to return to Jerusalem.

Meanwhile, life in Europe was becoming increasingly difficult, and the Jews were blamed for anything which went wrong. If a fire burned down a village, it was their fault. If a plague descended on a town, the Jews were accused of starting it in order to kill Christians. If someone were murdered, well, surely the Jews did it. Did an enemy invade the country? Why, the Jews had encouraged them to do so. If the people rebelled against the king, then both sides would plunder and rob the Jews – since the king accused the Jews of being rebels and the rebels accused the Jews of aiding the king. In addition to all this, every religious holiday – be it Easter, Christmas or Good Friday – was an excuse to cause suffering to the 'unbelieving' Jews.

Elsewhere, things were even worse. For example, in 1144 a young English boy, William of Norwich, disappeared. Soon, the general populace came to believe that the Jews had killed him in honour of Passover. After all, they claimed, there is a Jewish law which requires a Christian to be killed every year before Passover as a sacrifice. Ridiculous as the charge was, many people believed it. The Jews of Norwich were beaten and tortured, and some were even killed. Similar massacres took place in France and Germany, while in Spain the Muslim leaders forced some Jews to accept the Muslim faith.

It was very clear to some that the Jews, who had wandered all over the face of Europe in search of a resting place, had only one home, Eretz Israel. And so it was that in the year 1211, three hundred of the leading Jewish scholars and rabbis of England, France, and Italy set out for the Holy Land. The journey was a long,

The legendary combat between the Muslim general Saladin (right) and the English Crusader leader Richard the Lionheart

tiring one. But they knew that the time had come to return, and that if they went perhaps the people would soon follow. Unfortunately, of the three hundred who left, only a handful finally arrived in the Land. After all, in the thirteenth century such a journey took three to six months. It meant slow and dangerous travel with horse-drawn carriages on land, endless miles of walking on foot, sleeping in the open, exposure to cold and rain and snow and oppressive heat, going without food, coming down with illness and disease, being robbed by highwaymen, and being tormented and murdered at will. Those who could afford it went to an Italian coastal town such as Naples, and there boarded a vessel to Jaffa. Others took the overland route through Europe, into Turkey, then to Aleppo and Damascus in Syria, and finally into the city of their dreams, Jerusalem. Like so many thousands before them and after them, they came up the hill, tore their clothes as a sign of mourning, touched me, and prayed at my feet.

Those who did arrive at my shores did not find life easy, of course. The Holy Land was still a battleground. Many foreign countries and religions wanted to take her over, and for generations the Christians and Muslims, the Egyptians, Mongols and Turks fought against each other for the right to the land. Some, because they hated me, even tried to bury me, the Wall. I watched all this silently. I am old and I am patient, and I knew that only God's people can rule in God's land.

The thirteenth century was one of the most difficult for me to witness. As if the Crusaders had not done enough damage, the Mongols invaded in the year 1260. Once again the impoverished Jews of Jerusalem were slaughtered, their humble dwellings destroyed. Once again those who were fortunate enough managed to escape by doing what their fathers and grandfathers had done: they fled to the countryside and to the smaller towns of the Land.

But God has a way of providing for His people, and even in those difficult years, good things also happened. For example, one of the most famous sons of my people, the great Rabbi Moses ben Nahman – known as Nahmanides – lived in Gerona, that town in Spain which gave birth to so many great Jewish scholars in the Middle Ages. Nahmanides was the outstanding Jew of the thirteenth century. When he was only twenty he had begun publishing his commentaries and explanations on the Torah and Talmud. In addition to his Jewish learning, he was also trained in medicine, science, astronomy and mathematics. Whenever the Church ordered

LEFT 13th-century map of the Holy Land showing sailing ships making for harbour

BELOW Alfonso de Espina, an early leader of the Spanish Inquisition. The Jews behind him are shown blindfold, 'because they refuse to see the truth'. In medieval woodcuts, like the one on p. 148, Jews are often shown wearing pointed hats. In most places they had to wear some such different clothing to mark them out from the Christian population

public debates to be held against Judaism, it was always Nahmanides who was chosen to uphold the Jewish position. He defended it so well that after a debate against two hundred and fifty Christians in 1263, King James of Aragon declared him the winner. The Church raised such a storm of protest that he was forced to go into exile. Although Gerona had been comfortable, and Nahmanides knew that life in Eretz Israel was hard, he resolved to go there, to his spiritual home. In 1267, on the ninth of Elul, he arrived in Jerusalem.

He found that the Mongols had almost completely devastated the Holy City. Wherever he walked, he saw ruined buildings, poverty, destruction, He found a handful of Jews who supported themselves by making dye colours. The rest, perhaps fifteen families in all, were paupers and beggars. The synagogues had been destroyed and the Torah scrolls had either been burned or carried away by those Jews who had managed to escape.

Nahmanides was not only a great scholar, he was also a man of action. He gathered together the remaining Jews of Jerusalem and they decided to erect a synagogue and a house of study. They lovingly rebuilt one of the destroyed homes and transformed it into a place of prayer and Torah learning. He sent for the Torah scrolls which were being housed in Shechem, north of Jerusalem, and had them brought back. In the synagogue building he opened a school for study of Torah and Talmud. Soon young students from the entire region, even from hundreds of miles away, were attracted by the reputation and wisdom of the great rabbi. On the holidays, Jewish pilgrims from as far away as Damascus and Aleppo would come to Jerusalem and worship at the synagogue which Nahmanides built. And, of course, they would come up to me, the Western Wall, and there at my feet they would mourn the lost Temple, the ancient glory of the House of God.

Nahmanides was responsible for the return of many Jews to my land. He accomplished it all in a brief span of time, for he died in 1270 after living only three years in Palestine. But in his short stay, he brought new hope and courage to Jews all over the world: they were reminded once again that the Holy Land was waiting patiently for them.

The example of Nahmanides encouraged others to come, and by 1350 Eretz Israel could boast of Jews from Europe as well as from African and Asian lands. Kurdistan, Yemen, and Egypt all sent a small but steady flow of Jews, and Jerusalem which now had one hundred Jewish families – was the home of Jewish physicians, astronomers, and mathematicians as well as dyers, tailors and cobblers. Many of Jerusalem's Jews, however, were neither merchants nor professionals, but students of the Torah and of the mystical Kabbalah (see pp. 68–81). Other Jews were very proud of these scholars and righteous men, and gladly gave them money with which to continue their holy studies.

The one hundred Jewish families in Jerusalem were soon to grow in numbers – but for an unfortunate reason. About the year 1400, the Jews in Spain began to feel the bitter hatred of the priesthood and of popular uprisings which were aimed at forcing them to become Christians. Many, trying to save their lives, became Marranos – hidden Jews. In public, they behaved like Christians, but in private they maintained their Jewishness as best they could: *Sabbath, kashrut,* prayers, the holidays – all were kept in secret (see also p. 148).

Other Jews fled from Spain to the one place they could call home, the Land of Israel, and many settled in Jerusalem – where the Jews were all poor, and anyone who was able to eat bread regularly was considered a rich man. In addition, the Jews (like the Christians) were heavily taxed by the Muslim governor of Jerusalem: thirty-two pieces of silver – an enormous amount of money – had to be given as a head tax by each Jew. From time to time they were attacked by bands of marauders. In 1474, in fact, an angry mob

The Western Wall today

Kurdish Jews from Iran kissing the ground when they first arrived in Israel

burned down the beautiful Hurvah synagogue in Jerusalem.

This is one of the great miracles of all history: the fact that the Jews, despite so many troubles, continued to come to the Land. In 1428, for example, the Pope had decreed that it was forbidden for any Italian ships to transport Jews to the Holy Land. And then in 1468 he issued the same decree not only for Italian ships, but for any Christian ship. The Jews, as always, were considered unbelievers and unworthy, and it would be a sin, said the Pope, to help them return to the Holy Land.

As always, however, the attraction of Eretz Israel for the Jews was too powerful. If the seas were closed to them, they would travel the overland routes.

Many Jews literally walked to the Promised Land. Cities such as Nuremburg in Germany; Posen, Lublin and Lemberg in eastern Europe; Akerman, on the shores of the Black Sea; Samsun in Turkey; Aleppo and Damascus in Syria – all these cities were

An Ottoman monument in front of the Dome of the Rock, which stands on the site of the Temple in Jerusalem

stopping points as the Jews went in caravans to the land of their fathers.

One of the most famous to come was Rabbi Obadiah, who arrived in Jerusalem just prior to the Passover in 1488, after a long and hazardous journey from his home in the Italian town of Bertinoro. Rabbi Obadiah had already begun his famous explanation of the Mishnah, which is still used today by Jews all over the world. But in Jerusalem, in order to earn a livelihood and to be able to continue to study and write, he went to work as a gravedigger. He was proud of what he did, because it enabled him to live in the city of his dreams and to serve the people of Jerusalem. Although he had no special synagogue of his own, everyone considered him to be the most learned rabbi of Jerusalem. Obadiah of Bertinoro gave strength and inspiration to the Jews of Eretz Israel. He died in 1500 and was deeply mourned by Jews throughout the world.

By 1521, there were over five hundred families living in Jerusa-

Rabbi Zvi Hirsch Kalischer

lem. Jerusalem now no longer belonged to the Egyptians but to the Ottoman Turks, who had captured it from the Egyptians in 1517. (The Ottoman government ruled over Jerusalem for four hundred years, until 1917. Most of the walls of the Old City which we know today were rebuilt by the Turks in the sixteenth century.)

It was not only Jerusalem which was now beginning to develop. The cities which had had very few Jewish inhabitants since the Crusaders destroyed them – such as Acre, Jaffa, and Safed – began to attract many new settlers. Jewish mystics in particular were drawn to Safed. The majesty of its location – in the hills of Galilee – and the quiet beauty of its surroundings brought to it many of the great personalities of Kabbalah and mysticism. Rabbi Joseph Caro, the author of the Code of Jewish Law (the *Shulchan Arukh*), and Rabbi Isaac Luria, one of the greatest mystical scholars of all time, were just two of the dozens of saintly men who came from Europe and Africa to settle in Safed in the sixteenth century. They believed that the Messiah would soon come to redeem all Israel, and they wanted to be on holy soil when that day arrived.

Of course, Jews had always believed in the Messiah, but in the seventeenth century this belief reached such a peak that thousands of Jews from all over the world made their way to the Land. There they waited for the arrival of God's appointed messenger who would bring all the Jews back to their home and would usher in true peace among all men.

By the end of the eighteenth century there were over five thousand Jews in Eretz Israel, and most of these lived in Jerusalem. These Jews prayed every single day for the coming of the Messiah. And in 1798, when Napoleon conquered Egypt and part of the Holy Land, some thought that this was a sign that the Messiah would soon arrive.

Life in the Land was unchanged. There were periods of quiet, in which Jews were not disturbed by the country's rulers. But there were other times when the old persecutions took place again. I wept silently as I witnessed certain criminal acts against my faithful people. For example, in 1621, the government, for no reason, imprisoned the rabbis and scholars of Jerusalem, and imposed heavy taxes on all the Jews. In 1720, a number of Arabs broke into one of the fine synagogues in Jerusalem, set it afire, and forced all the Jews in the neighbourhood to abandon their homes for fear of their lives.

There were personal tragedies as well. The famous Rabbi Judah Hasid had left Poland in 1699 together with thirteen hundred of his disciples. Their destination: Jerusalem, of course. But weakened by the journey, he died just after he arrived in Jerusalem. His disciples, without their leader, suffered much torment, were often thrown into prison without cause, and suffered many indignities at the hands of the Turkish inhabitants of Jerusalem. Despite all this, one of Rabbi Judah's disciples, a Rabbi Gedaliah, wrote that:

It is a rare delight to dwell in the Land of Israel . . . we are able to fulfil commandments that can only be done in the land . . . we have no other occupation than to study and pray by day and by night. May the words of the prophet Isaiah (35:10) be fulfilled for us speedily in our days: 'And the ransomed of the Lord shall return and come to Zion with song, with everlasting joy upon their head; gladness and joy shall they obtain, and sorrow and sighing shall flee away.'

A few years after Rabbi Judah Hasid's journey, the famous Rabbi Moses Hayyim Luzzato met a similar fate. After a lifetime of wandering through the various European countries he decided finally to make his own journey to the Land. But as was true for so many others, the journey was so difficult that he died from disease soon after he landed in 1747.

Although my people remained faithful to me through the centuries, the years of suffering and wandering and tragedy began to show their mark on some of them. There were European Jews, especially in the eighteenth century, who began to lose all hope of ever returning to the Land. Perhaps, they thought, the best solution to the troubles of the Jews would be for them to assimilate, to become just like the gentiles around them. This attitude gained some popularity after the French Revolution, when all Jews in France were granted complete rights as citizens. This was in 1791. Similar equality was granted a few years later in Holland, in Germany, and Austria. For a short time, it seemed that the Messiah had indeed arrived – and that he had come not to the Holy Land but to Europe.

These freedoms, however, were soon eroded; and the largest numbers of Jews lived farther east, in Russia, where the plight of the Jews was worse than ever. When it became clear that even in the rest of Europe the new freedoms were only temporary, a new fervour and longing for the Promised Land developed. Every people had its own land, they reasoned; surely Jews must have their own land in Eretz Israel.

In 1862, Rabbi Zevi Hirsch Kalischer from the town of Thorn in eastern Europe published a pamphlet calling on all Jews to settle in Israel. Our people, he wrote, must return to their ancient homeland, and till the soil, work the fields, study the Torah, and gradually rebuild the Land with their own hands. As a result of Rabbi Kalischer's efforts, renewed impetus was given to the return to Zion, and an agricultural school, Mikveh Yisrael, was opened near Jaffa (see also pp. 177–8).

About this time, Polish and Russian Jews endured severe pogroms and persecutions. For example, scores of Jews were wounded and killed in Poland on Christmas day in 1880. And on Easter Monday of 1882, in Podolia, Russia, hundreds of Jews were wounded, forty killed, fifteen hundred Jewish shops and dwellings destroyed, and fifteen thousand were left homeless.

While many then left for the United States, a number of young Russian and Polish Jews organized themselves into groups and

First sight of the Holy Land

went to Israel together. Some went to Mikveh Yisrael; others to Rishon le-Zion, Gederah, and Petach Tikvah – all newly founded settlements. The story of how they fought the difficult conditions – the climate, the unyielding soil, the enmity of the Arabs, the barren countryside, the malaria-infested swamps – forms one of the great and heroic chapters of human courage. For one thing they felt very clearly: they no longer could be guests in the lands of the Exile. They wanted to go home. Fired with pride in their Jewishness, they knew that ultimately an independent Jewish state must be reborn on this ancient soil. Even though it seemed like an impossible dream, they had the vision to see that the Land – and I – had been waiting patiently for two thousand years for their return, for the establishment of a government of Jews to rule the Jewish land. Some called this modern Zionism. As for me, I knew that it was the natural result of the ancient and stubborn faith of my people.

I knew now that it would not be long before my Jews would stream back to me not in the hundreds but in the tens of thousands. For I am the great symbol of the Land – the Wall – and I knew that because my children had never abandoned me, the stage was now set for the dramatic events of the coming twentieth century – a century which would see both the tragedy of the destruction of Europe's Jews, and the triumph of a Jewish flag fluttering over the Jewish city of holiness, the city of Jerusalem.

EMANUEL FELDMAN

OPPOSITE AND ABOVE Two of the earliest pioneering settlements in the land of Israel, Mikveh Israel agricultural school (opposite) and Rishon-le-Zion (above), at the beginning of this century

LEFT Returning home after prayers at the Western Wall

The Wrong Answer

It is told:

When Rabbi Wolf Kitzes took leave of his teacher, before setting out for the Holy Land, the Baal Shem stretched out his second finger, touched him on the mouth, and said: 'Heed your words, and see to it that you give the right reply!' He refused to say anything more.

The ship of which the Baal Shem's[*] disciple had taken passage was driven from its course by a tempest, and forced to land on an unknown, and apparently desert island. Presently the storm died down, but the vessel had suffered damage and could not put out to sea again immediately. Some of the passengers, Rabbi Wolf among them, went ashore to have a look at the unfamiliar foreign landscape. The others turned back after a while, but he was so deep in meditation that he went on and on and finally came to a big house built in an old-fashioned style, which looked as if no one had ever lived in it. Only then did he remember that the ship would not wait for him, but before he could decide one way or another, a man in a linen garment appeared on the threshold. His features were age-old, his hair was white, but he bore himself erect. 'Do not be afraid, Rabbi Wolf,' he said. 'Spend the sabbath with us. The morning after you will be able to resume your journey.' As in a dream, Rabbi Wolf followed the old man to the bath, prayed in the company of ten tall majestic old men, and ate with them. The sabbath passed as in a dream. The next morning, the age-old man accompanied him down to the shore where his ship was lying at anchor, and blessed him in parting. But just as Rabbi Wolf was hurrying to set foot on the gangplank, his host asked him: 'Tell me, Rabbi Wolf: How do the Jews fare in your country?'

[*]The Baal Shem Tov, Israel ben Eliezer, was the founder of *Hasidism*. For more about him, see p. 80.

'The Lord of the world does not abandon them,' Rabbi Wolf replied quickly and walked on. Not until he was on the high seas,
did his mind clear. Then he recalled the words of his teacher and
was seized with such bitter remorse that he resolved not to continue
his voyage to the Holy Land, but to go home at once. He spoke to
one of the crew and gathered from his reply that he was already
homeward bound.

When Rabbi Wolf came to the Baal Shem, his master looked at
him sorrowfully but not angrily and said: 'That was the wrong
answer you gave to our father Abraham! Day after day he asks
God: "How are my children?" And God replies: "I do not abandon
them." If only you had told him of the sufferings of exile!'

MARTIN BUBER

The ship was driven from its course by a
tempest

The Realization of the Dream

With the growth of the concept of nationalism in the mid-nineteenth century, Jewish yearning to return to the homeland crystallized into a political philosophy. Although some small groups had already settled in Eretz Israel, the political movement, known as Zionism, was really created by one man, Theodor Herzl. His was the inspiration and his the energy which gave the impetus to the movement. Its first great political success – the Balfour Declaration – was also largely the result of the untiring efforts of one man, Chaim Weizmann. In no more than fifty years, a period of alternating hope and disappointment, the seemingly impractical dream became a reality, and the state of Israel came into being.

The Forerunners

The story of the emergence and success, within a relatively short span of time, of the political movement aimed at re-establishing the Jews as a sovereign people in their ancestral home is so astonishing that it is tempting to portray the leaders of this movement, known as Zionism, as knights charging forward to victory, armed only with the rightness of their cause. But Zionism is a part of history, and history is a messy business. Add to that the fact that the land of Israel, the home of the Jews, was a focus of the ambitions of the super-powers of the early twentieth century, and it becomes clear that the story is bound to seem even more confused.

It is rather commonly assumed that the driving force of the Jewish desire to return to the land of Israel was anti-Semitism. In other words, that when the host-societies pressed harder on the Jews than was their traditional custom then the Jews woke up and said, 'This is intolerable. We must have our own country.' However, this is not correct. It is true that anti-Semitism was a remarkably sturdy weed, finding new, pseudo-scientific soil in which to grow when rationalism undermined the old religious basis of Jew-hatred.

But the early visionaries of Zionism did not merely react against discrimination; they gave new life to an ancient hope. As you will have seen from the chapter 'The Dream of the Return', the link between Israel and the widely scattered Jewish communities was never broken. Over the centuries Jews continued to undertake dangerous journeys to settle in the land they considered their own, no matter who was ruling the area at the time. Time and again war and disease killed many of them. Yet they kept on coming. Messianic fervour moved them in many different places and at many different times to follow leaders, some warlike, some peaceable, most sincere,

OPPOSITE A typical street scene in Tel Aviv, Israel's largest city

OPPOSITE Excavating under the Western Wall today

some charlatans, who claimed to be precursors of the Messiah (or even the Messiah himself), come to lead the people of Israel back to the Holy Land. Nowadays many people find this kind of enthusiasm hard to understand, and even objectionable, for they wish to be thought sensible people, but for eighteen centuries Jewish communities flocked eagerly to listen to men or women who proclaimed that it was their mission to lead them home.

A few examples will suffice. The first messianic leaders were guerrilla fighters against Roman rule in the first century CE. Best known of these were the Zealots, who probably first made their appearance around 6 CE. Around the same time there were leaders whose aims may not have been political but whose followers certainly regarded them as nationalistic leaders. Chief of these was Jesus of Nazareth, who chose a Zealot called Simon for one of his disciples and who was thought a sufficient danger to security for him to be executed by the Romans. The leaders of the great Jewish revolts of 66–70 CE (see pp. 144–5) and 132–35 CE were seen in messianic terms, particularly Simeon Bar Kokhba (see p. 116). Other messianic claimants appeared in Crete in 448, in Iraq around 645, in Iran at the end of the seventh century, in Salonika in 1096 and throughout Europe in the first half of the twelfth century. A scholar named Moses proclaimed the coming of the Messiah in Fez, Morocco, in the 1120s, a prophetess emerged in Baghdad in 1121, and a few years later David Alroy led a remarkable, and probably armed, messianic uprising in Kurdistan. In Spain in particular messianic hopes were frequently raised in the twelfth to fifteenth centuries.

The next century saw the great ferment engendered in Jewish communities in Italy, Portugal and Turkey by David Reuveni and Solomon Molcho. Almost all Jewish communities, especially those in Poland-Lithuania, were stirred by the advent of the pseudo-Messiah Shabbetai Zevi in the 1660s. His conversion to Islam under fear of punishment shattered the movement, dealing a great blow to popular messianic beliefs.

The concept of a Messiah who would lead the Jewish people back to their home became internalized, particularly through Hasidism (see pp. 80–1). Zevi Hirsch Kalischer, however, rabbi of Posen, came to the opinion, which he first expressed in his book *Drishat Zion* in 1836, that the Jews must not wait for a Messiah but must take active steps to establish themselves in the Holy Land. Agricultural settlements, owned and worked by Jews, were to be the basis of this return, not charitable activities. The first project owing its inspiration to Kalischer's efforts was the Mikveh Israel agricultural school, which opened in 1870.

The nineteenth century saw a number of proposals for a return of the Jews to the Holy Land, or for the establishment of a Jewish state, ranging from Napoleon's appeal to the Jews of Asia and Africa to help him restore Jerusalem, to the American judge

Shabbetai Zevi, leader of a popular Jewish messianic movement in 17th-century Europe and the Middle East

Manuel Noah who wanted to set up a Jewish state near Buffalo. An independent Jewish presence in Palestine, forming a corridor between Turks and Egyptians, was considered by the British Foreign Office as early as 1838. Similar projects, stemming from gentiles and Jews, were put forward in Germany and Britain in the 1840s. But the one with the greatest impact was a book by Moses Hess.

During the nineteenth century Jews living in western Europe were gradually emancipated, and at least legally became full citizens of the countries in which they lived. Many then turned away from Judaism, leaving it behind in the ghetto, and concentrated on becoming accepted as Germans, Frenchmen, etc. Moses Hess, who was born in Germany in 1812, was such a man, an active socialist and former colleague of Marx and Engels. Surprising his contemporaries, he published in 1862 a work called *Rome and Jerusalem* which begins with the words, 'After twenty years of estrangement I have returned to my people.' At a time when most German Jews looked forward to increasing assimilation, Moses Hess declared, 'We shall always remain strangers among the nations.' The only solution was a Jewish state in Israel.

On neither religious nor secular Jewry did Kalischer's book *Drishat Zion* nor Hess's *Rome and Jerusalem* have any marked immediate effect.

In eastern Europe, where the greatest majority of the world's Jews then lived, the late nineteenth century was a dismal period. New anti-Semitic laws and an increasing number of pogroms exacerbated the poverty and misery which two American immigration officers said in 1892 was the worst they had ever seen in their lives. Tiring of necessarily feeble efforts to better this situation, in 1882 Leon Pinsker, a doctor living in Odessa, published *Auto-Emancipation*, an impassioned appeal to have done with protests against anti-Semitism, which he saw as a hereditary and incurable aberration. The Jews should cease to be strangers everywhere and acquire their own home.

None of these three men knew of the work of the others, but small groups known as Hovevei Zion ('Lovers of Zion') had sprung up, inspired by such visions, and agricultural settlements were set up in Rishon le-Zion, Petach Tikvah and Gederah. The Lovers of Zion came mainly from Russia and their arrival in Constantinople seeking entry permits to Palestine (then part of the Turkish Ottoman empire) was looked on with great suspicion by the Turkish authorities, who banned the immigration of Russian Jews in 1893. These difficulties were overcome when land was bought by western European Jews and local officials were discreetly bribed, but obviously such conditions could permit only a few settlements to be established. Hovevei Zion was therefore a minor movement, although small groups were established throughout the whole of Europe, especially eastern Europe.

The Movement

Zionism proper begins with the publication in Vienna in 1896 of *Der Judenstaat* (The Jewish State) by Theodor Herzl. In it the thirty-six-year-old Herzl, a foreign correspondent of note and author of respected plays and essays – in fact the very picture of the assimilated western European Jew – stated roundly that assimilation had not been successful and could not be. Without having read Pinsker he reached the same conclusion: the Jews must have their own country. At first he contemplated Argentina, but soon came to believe that the land of Israel, the never-forgotten historic homeland, was the only possible place. Gradual colonization, of the type undertaken by Hovevei Zion, would only lead to a reaction on the part of the non-Jewish population. The right of the Jews to their own land must be guaranteed by international sanctions. 'To achieve this,' said Herzl, 'we require diplomatic negotiations . . . and propaganda on the largest scale.'

The few Zionists already in existence derided Herzl's book, for he was so obviously ignorant of any moves made so far. But they mistook the man. Herzl was not simply a visionary; he was a man of tireless energy. He set out for Constantinople in an effort to persuade the sultan's advisers to give Palestine to the Jews as a vassal state in return for large loans (which he had no certain way of raising). The Turks were polite, but not interested in giving away to anyone any part of the Ottoman empire. Herzl made further trips to the pope, the German emperor and leaders in Italy, Britain and Russia. Leading Jewish figures received him doubtfully, but news of his mission inspired the masses in many places.

With his earliest supporters, David Wolffsohn and Max Nordau, Herzl set about organizing a movement. A newspaper, *Die Welt*, was first published in June 1897 and the first Zionist congress opened in Basel, Switzerland, on 29 August of the same year. After discussion and dissension, the congress had decided to accept as its platform that 'Zionism seeks to secure for the Jewish people a publicly, recognized, legally secured home in Palestine.' The first Zionist congress aroused great interest, enthusiasm and distrust, but it also achieved Herzl's aim of publicizing the movement widely. Fifty years after this first congress, Herzl wrote in his diary, the Jewish state would be born. Other Zionist leaders were far less optimistic, but in fact exactly fifty years later the United Nations passed the resolution that made Israel a political reality and the state was proclaimed a few months later.

The second Zionist congress, a year later, was attended by Chaim Weizmann, a scientist from Russia. He was impressed by Herzl's fervour, but doubted his practical abilities. Annual congresses took place, and fund-raising was attempted, while Herzl made fruitless attempts to get a direct answer from the sultan, and tried to enlist English or German support. From the outset there were

RIGHT Moses Hess

BELOW Theodor Herzl and other members
of the Zionist mission aboard ship on
their way to meet the Kaiser in 1898

OPPOSITE ABOVE LEFT Sultan Abdul
Hamid II, Ottoman emperor and ruler of
Palestine until 1909

OPPOSITE ABOVE RIGHT
David Wolffsohn

OPPOSITE BELOW Herzl with his mother
in 1902

The building in Basle, Switzerland, where the first Zionist congress met in 1897

dissensions within the movement, some delegates resenting what they considered the 'interference' of the rabbis, others deeply suspicious of the socialists. The biggest storm, which almost split the movement, broke at the sixth congress, when Herzl put forward the British proposal for Jewish settlement in Uganda. Although Herzl pushed the Uganda scheme through, affirming that it was only an interim solution, opposition to it was so fierce, especially in eastern Europe, that it faded and was officially declared dead at the seventh congress in 1904. Herzl himself died before this, on 3 July 1904.

However, the movement did not die with him, as many had perhaps expected. David Wolffsohn took over as president. Negotiations with Turkey continued, but the movement simply did not have the money for impressive diplomatic manoeuvres. In spite of Turkish policy, a second wave of immigration, mainly from Russia, took place in 1904. By 1914 there were about 80,000 Jews in Palestine; Tel Aviv had been founded; different kinds of agricultural collectives were set up; and a Hebrew secondary school, technical institute and art museum were established.

With the outbreak of World War I in 1914, Zionism entered the international political stage. The prospect of the end of the Ottoman empire set Britain and France (although allies) and Germany scrambling for power in the Middle East. Deluded by their own propaganda, the Powers overestimated Jewish influence as a whole and the Zionist movement in particular. The London *Times*, Britain's most prestigious newspaper, considered Zionism essentially a 'German' movement, and a number of meetings which took place between Zionist and German leaders in Germany may have induced the British Foreign Office to fear that Germany would rally to the cause of a Jewish Palestine. It was hardly in the interests of the Germans to upset their Turkish allies by sponsoring such a state, but the British government seems to have been seriously alarmed by the prospect. In fact the Zionist leadership was thrown into disarray with the leaders in Berlin unable to liaise with Weizman in Britain, who was exercising all his considerable powers of persuasion to win adherents to his cause in the British government. Most Zionists can only have been surprised when, on 2 November 1917, Arthur Balfour, the British Secretary of State for Foreign Affairs, declared in a letter to Lord Rothschild:

'His Majesty's Government view with favour the establishment in Palestine of a national home for the Jewish people, and will use their best endeavours to facilitate the achievement of this object, it being clearly understood that nothing shall be done which may prejudice the civil and religious rights of the existing non-Jewish communities in Palestine, or the rights and political status enjoyed by Jews in any other country.'

Many reasons have been put forward to explain this step. It has been represented as a Machiavellian move by the British to extend their sphere of interest in the Middle East (they were already in virtual control of Egypt), and such considerations undoubtedly played a part. But self-interest is not a sufficient answer. Balfour himself, like not a few leaders of his day, was deeply religious, believed sincerely in the Bible, and regarded the return of the Jewish people to the Holy Land as the fulfilment of biblical prophecy. Though there is little to suggest that he either knew or liked personally many Jews, he thought that they were the most gifted race on earth since the ancient Greeks and that Christianity owed them an incalculable debt.

In the meantime other agreements were afoot. The British High

Members of the Zionist Commission arrive in Palestine in April 1918

Commissioner in Egypt, Sir Henry McMahon, enlisting the aid of the Arabs in the Franco-British struggle to expel the Turks, agreed with the Sharif Hussain of Mecca that the latter should organize an Arab revolt to get rid of the Turks in return for British recognition of Arab independence in the vast regions where until then Arabs were under foreign rule. To complicate matters further, in 1916, Sir Mark Sykes of the British Foreign Office signed an agreement with his French counterpart, Charles Georges Picot, which divided much of the Arab world into British and French spheres of influence (Russia ratified this). Palestine, apart from north of Acre, was to be British and Jerusalem was to be part of a vaguely envisaged international zone.

Obviously, these three agreements could not be reconciled, but astonishing though it seems to us now, Sykes himself was a fervent supporter of both Arab and Jewish nationalism and believed that they would collaborate. It seems true to say that the British and French had no doubt that they were living in a Europe-centred world, believed the ambitions of each other and of Germany to be of prior importance, and vaguely assumed that all lesser matters would straighten themselves out in time. It is worth noting that Balfour himself wrote in 1919:

'so far as Palestine is concerned, the Powers have made no statement of fact that is not admittedly wrong, and no declaration of policy which, at least in the letter, they have not always intended to violate.'

Vague and contradictory though it was, the Balfour Declaration was supported by the United States, and ratified by all the Allied

OPPOSITE Arthur Balfour in Tel Aviv. On far right of the photograph is Sokolow and beside him, in profile, stands Chaim Weizmann

LEFT British rule over Palestine began with General Allenby's official entry into Jerusalem

BELOW Faisal with Lawrence of Arabia (centre). Lawrence's promises to Faisal further complicated the situation in the Middle East

185

Haj Amin al-Hussaini, the Grand Mufti of Jerusalem (a title invented by the British)

Powers in 1920, Lloyd George, the British prime minister, saying to Weizman at the time, 'Now you have your state.' Two years later the British Mandate was confirmed by the League of Nations. There was a new and larger wave of Jewish immigrants and the country began to prosper. Attracted by such prosperity, numbers of Arabs came to Palestine from neighbouring areas.

The Arabs

At first it even seemed as if Sykes might be right. The leader of the Arab delegation to the post-war peace conference, Faisal, son of Sharif Hussain, said in a published statement in December 1918: 'The two main branches of the semitic family, Arabs and Jews, understand one another and I hope that as a result of the interchange of ideas at the Peace Conference each nation will make definite progress towards the realization of its aspirations. Arabs are not jealous of Zionist Jews and intend to give them fair play, but the Zionist Jews have assured the nationalist Arabs of their intention to see that they too have fair play in their respective areas.'

But this was little more than a moment of friendship. One very common statement about Palestine must first be dealt with. The early Zionists did not think that they were coming to an empty country. They were perfectly well aware of the Arab population. While most of the early Russian Zionists felt sure that Jews and Arabs could live together in peace, Ahad Ha'am, the great exponent of cultural Zionism, felt in 1891 that the Arabs would soon begin to notice, and resent, a significant increase in the Jewish presence. And there were indeed frequent, and sometimes bloody, encounters between the Arabs and the early immigrants. Arab protests first took written form with a letter from a group of Jerusalem notables to Constantinople in 1891. Arab nationalism as such was only allowed a voice after the fall of Sultan Abdul Hamid in 1908 and an apparent change in Turkish policy. Objections to Zionism were among the first ideas to be voiced. Their own Jews the Arabs were used to. Islam tolerated them to a greater extent than Christianity, but they were a second-class people and generally despised. The new Jews were an object of suspicion and fear. In their turn, the Jewish pioneers did not understand the Arabs; while generally hoping that all would go well, some also despised a people whose ways were so different from their own. Ironically, their very socialism prevented co-operation, for the early settlers were determined that the Jews themselves must be workers, and would gain respect for their industry and evident ability to defend themselves. Before 1914 there were, however, occasional efforts at political co-operation, instigated by both parties, in the towns and cities.

In the outside Arab world, the Balfour Declaration was received with mild friendship, Arab speakers appearing on a Zionist platform in London and important newspapers in Cairo and Mecca welcoming the return of 'the original sons of the country'. Previous misunderstandings, both sides agreed, had been the fault of the Turks. Faisal and Weizmann signed an agreement in which Faisal waived Arab claims to Palestine. However, Faisal added a postscript making it clear that the agreement stood only if the British granted the Arabs in other countries the independence they had been promised.

Understandably, the Zionists overrated the importance of statements made in Cairo and Mecca and agreements signed by Faisal. In the first place, it soon became clear that Arab aspirations were not going to be met by the colonial powers. Secondly, the Arabs in Palestine did not in the least consider Faisal their spokesman and protested openly against the Balfour Declaration. That the first British High Commissioner, Sir Herbert Samuel, was a Jew, did nothing to allay their fears (although as far as he was concerned these fears were misplaced; in his efforts to be fair to both sides, Samuel greatly angered the Zionists). Resistance culminated in riots in 1920–21.

In 1921, Palestine was partitioned. Transjordan was the name given to that part of Palestine which lies beyond the Jordan to the east and which constituted about three-quarters of the area of the original British mandate. The articles in the Palestine mandate relating to the Jewish National Home were no longer to apply to Transjordan and it was closed to Jewish settlement, although otherwise remaining under British protection.

The founding meeting of Jabotinsky's Revisionists, Paris, 1925

For the next eight years or so, the country was relatively quiet and at the Zionist congresses the delegates continued to insist, with sincerity, on their desire to live at peace with the Arabs. Riots broke out again in 1929 and 1933 and civil war in 1936. It is frequently stated that Haj Amin al-Husseini, member of a leading Palestinian family who was appointed *mufti* (religious leader and representative of the Muslim community) of Jerusalem by Sir Herbert Samuel, was the instigator of all this trouble. Haj Amin was a demagogue and a fanatic, but it may be doubted if his influence alone was enough to stir a quiescent people. In truth, the Zionists did not at first understand the full force of Arab nationalist feelings, being convinced that the bulk of the population wanted economic betterment, not a political voice. The Labour Zionists tended to think that one or another European government lay behind Arab uprisings and that anyway the Arab leaders in no way represented the Arab workers (a mistake they still make). After the 1929 riots only the Revisionists (Jabotinsky's breakaway Zionist group) recognized that the Arabs, true patriots themselves, fully understood the Zionist aims and naturally resisted them. Conflict between Jews and Arabs, however regrettable, was inevitable.

By the time of the 1936 rebellion, little hope for co-operation remained. Driven by the deepening shadow of Nazi rule, over 130,000 new Jewish immigrants had arrived in the country. Between

ABOVE Muslim propaganda, warning of the threat of a Zionist invasion of the whole Middle East. Probably distributed by supporters of Haj Amin al-Hussaini, since he is shown as ruler of Jerusalem

OPPOSITE ABOVE Ha-Shomer (the watchman), the early Jewish defence group

OPPOSITE BELOW Haganah troops in 1941

189

1933 and 1939 it gradually became evident that European Jews faced the prospect of ruin and death, not only individually but as a people. No country in the world (except the Dominican Republic, at Evian in July 1938) came forward with a positive offer of assistance to Hitler's victims. Is it any wonder that Palestine looked like the only refuge and that considerations of internal problems were put aside?

The Mandatory Authorities

In the meantime, the British government vacillated. The notions of strict fairness, British type, which inspired the military administration from December 1917 until June 1920 (no treaty having been signed with the Turks, the country was officially occupied enemy territory), were almost laughably inappropriate and succeeded only in angering both Arabs and Zionists. There is no reason to believe that the British military administration was pro-Arab, but they certainly misunderstood (and probably disliked) the predominantly eastern European Zionists and at first even tried to avoid the publication of the Balfour Declaration in the hope that the problem would just go away.

Since many of the promises made to them by the European powers had not been honoured, the Arabs throughout the whole region believed that they had been duped, and doubly so in Palestine, so they too watched the actions of the British authorities with deep suspicion. The Zionist leaders, well aware that the British government was in several minds about the Balfour Declaration, were anxious to have the mandatory authorities commit themselves to support for Zionist aims.

After the riots of 1928, in which the British administration refused to allow Jewish defenders to arm themselves against savage Arab attacks throughout the country, the Zionists in Palestine no longer trusted the British. The entirely inadequate British police force was ineffectual and the Arab policemen stood aside when, as in Hebron, the mob attacked the 700-strong Jewish community, slaughtering and dismembering any man, woman or child they could lay hands on. The British Colonial Secretary, Lord Passfield, was unmoved and the upshot was the Shaw Commission, leading to the 1930 White Paper, which recommended restricting Jewish immigration and land purchase. The Peel Commission of 1937, sent out after the 1936 uprising, recommended further partition of the country as the only answer, as did the Woodhead Commission of 1938. Instead, in May 1939 the British government issued a White Paper rejecting partition, repudiating the notion of a Jewish state (or an Arab one) in western Palestine, limiting Jewish immigration to 75,000 in the next five years, after which it would stop unless the Arabs of Palestine wished otherwise. Jewish land purchase was also forbidden in some districts and restricted in others.

TOP Ernest Bevin, British Foreign Secretary in the post-war Labour government

ABOVE Harry S. Truman, President of the United States, 1945–53

OPPOSITE Jewish immigrants, refused permission to land, being deported to Cyprus. British soldiers scrutinize the crowd to see if it contains any Jews wanted for guerilla actions against the British

191

This White Paper was published soon after the German invasion of Czechoslovakia made the outbreak of war almost inevitable. Hunted on all sides, the Jews felt betrayed by the British whom, nevertheless, they were bound to support in a war against Germany. The mandatory government, during the first six months of World War II, refused to permit any Jewish immigration, at first imprisoning illegal immigrants and later transporting them elsewhere. Throughout the war they did not allow even the full permitted number of immigrants to enter. This was at a time when the authorities knew full well what happened to Jews who could not escape from Europe. At the same time the mandatory government tried to ignore any specifically Jewish war effort and disarmed and arrested members of Haganah, the defence organization. Jewish guerrilla groups proliferated, the more extreme considering Britain as an outright enemy. The Irgun Zvai Leumi, the largest of these, had a considerable amount of support within the Jewish community although the Jewish Agency tried hard to oppose acts which the British government naturally denounced as terrorism.

During the 1930s, American Zionism, previously fairly weak, rose in strength and funds, especially after the beginning of Nazi persecution. American unwillingness to admit Jewish refugees and the outbreak of the war turned American Jewry's attitude to Zionism from general indifference to impassioned support. President Roosevelt and his administration, however, were at best lukewarm. Throughout the world Jews became desperate. The Allies' chance to negotiate with the Nazis in order to save the Hungarian Jews was turned down. Jewish Agency appeals for the bombing of Auschwitz in order to delay the mass murders were dismissed as 'of . . . doubtful efficacy'. Yet only an Allied victory could save any survivors. The full horror of the death camps was revealed in April 1945. Around six out of every seven Jews living in Europe had died. The urgent necessity of a Jewish state seemed undeniable.

For the next three years bitterness between the Palestine Jewish community and the British government steadily increased. The new British Foreign Secretary, Ernest Bevin, while probably not anti-Semitic as some have claimed, had little liking for either Arabs or Jews and on balance was more strongly irritated by the latter. It is hard to believe that an otherwise humane man could respond to Jewish aspirations, at such a time in their history, with no warmer feeling than exasperation, but it is so. However, in the United States, President Truman had been won over to the Zionist cause. By another irony of history, the British feared that the largely socialist Jews in Palestine would turn towards the Soviet Union and thought that the Arabs were naturally inclined to be pro-western. Jewish refugees still remained in Displaced Person's camps while the victors haggled over where to allow them to go. In the face of mounting tension and increasing attacks on and by

OPPOSITE A synagogue in Safed, a most important holy place in the Land of Israel, home of Joseph Caro and Isaac Luria.

OPPOSITE Lake Galilee and Tiberias

British soldiers (for which each side has of course blamed the other ever since), support for one or other of the clandestine Jewish defence groups grew. The British government therefore decided in 1947 to lay the problem before the United Nations. To the surprise of the Zionists, the Soviet Union expressed sympathy and support. After months of deliberation, hearing all points of view, the United Nations Commission decided in favour of partition. After the plan was published, and grudgingly accepted by the United States, there was widespread Arab-Jewish violence. As the end of the Mandate, set for 14 May 1948, approached, fighting intensified, growing increasingly savage. The British duly left and the State of Israel was proclaimed at 4 p.m. on 14 May with David Ben Gurion as the first prime minister and Weizmann as the first president. As the countries of the United Nations, headed by the United States and seconded by the USSR, came forward to recognize the new state (and in effect acknowledge their sense of guilt), the Arab armies launched full-scale war.

The Refugees

By the end of the War of Independence, in January 1949, about 6,000 of Israel's 650,000 Jewish citizens were dead and around 500,000 of the 700,000 or so former Arab inhabitants of the country had left. Those who remained became citizens of Israel. Whether the Arabs simply fled because they found the battle-torn country temporarily intolerable, whether they were induced to leave by the Arab commanders, or whether they were actively incited to leave by Jewish harassment are points which have been bitterly contested ever since. A mass of conflicting statements have been made, based on a paucity of conflicting evidence. Whatever the reasons for their flight, about half a million Arabs, formerly resident in Palestine, were herded into refugee camps in the neighbouring Arab countires and there the majority have remained ever since, cared for largely by the United Nations. In December 1948 the United Nations General Assembly urged that, in the context of a negotiated peace between the belligerents, the 'refugees wishing to return to their homes and live at peace with their neighbours should be permitted to do so at the earliest practical date, and that compensation should be paid for property of those not choosing to return.' But no such peace settlement has yet been negotiated.

Israel, struggling to absorb penniless Jews, many of them from the increasingly hostile Arab countries, contended that the Arab governments deliberately kept the refugees in their camps as a political propaganda device. An Israeli offer, made in 1949, to readmit 100,000 refugees was rejected. The death of King Abdullah of Jordan in 1951 meant the end of the only serious effort on behalf of one of her neighbours to negotiate a peace with Israel.

David Ben Gurion proclaims the State of of Israel on 14 May 1948 in the Tel Aviv Museum

For their part, the Arab countries protested that the western world had paid its debt to the Jews at their expense and, although asserting that their enemy was Israel and not the Jews, they disseminated widely anti-Semitic propaganda on the western, and ultimately Christian, model. A new generation grew up in the camps, educated in hatred of Israel.

Had they been given the chance, numbers of Arab refugees of 1948–9 might have opted for compensation and citizenship of some neighbouring country in preference to return to a home under the rule of a people with whose aims they had naturally little sympathy. Now, however, the problem is of a different order. It may be correct to say that Palestinian nationalism was a minority concept in 1948, but now it definitely exists and no amount of wishing will make it go away. The refugee problem is no longer, if it ever was, simply a humanitarian one; it is a political problem. Among the many other serious difficulties (not least the designs of the super-powers) in the way of peace in the Middle East, account must be taken of Palestinian nationalism. Neither Israel nor the Arab countries can ignore the claims of the Palestinians, the more extreme of whom have made known, with dramatic and horrifying acts of terrorism, their determined hostility to Israel. Talk of a secular Palestine, or of a greater Israel in which all citizens, Jewish and Arab, will have equal rights, is wishful thinking. The increasing hatred on both sides will not simply wither away. Any settlement can only work if it gives full recognition to the seriously conflicting aspirations of Israel and the Palestinians.

The Present Day

After twenty-five years of statehood, and four major wars, Israel is a country justly proud of its achievements. The land supports more people, at a far higher standard of living, than was ever imagined by any except the early Zionist visionaries. Peaceful it is not, but the country is vibrant and relatively prosperous. Israel is a vociferous democracy, with a high standard of education and technology, and an unusual degree of social cohesion, despite many factional squabbles. The Israeli Arabs, though they have their legitimate grievances, are full citizens with their own representatives in parliament and educational autonomy to preserve their sense of national pride. The continuing conflict has, however, embittered relationships between Arab and Jew within Israel. The other large minority, the Druze, elected to serve in the Israeli army and have been among Israel's most determined advocates.

It was the aim of the early Zionists to 'normalize' the Jews by making them citizens of their own historic land. Did their heirs succeed in fulfilling this aim? Israel now has her own army, her own parliament, her own trade union movement and her own internal political quarrels, her own strikes, her own criminals. It is in all respects a 'normal' country – except one: the great majority of her citizens are Jews. Those gentiles who wish to give some cover of rationality to their need to hate Jews, now claim to hate only Zionists (but by their definition all Jews are Zionists). Those who once shrilly denounced a world Jewish conspiracy, now find evidence everywhere of a worldwide Zionist conspiracy. The same sort of people who regarded the Jews in the west as 'oriental' and therefore alien, now claim that the Jews in Israel are 'western' and therefore alien. Among those who loudly pronounce their support for the Arab cause are not a few who, on examination, have little liking for Arabs. Anti-Semitism has indeed declined – newer hatreds have often taken its place. But the great number of Jews living outside Israel, although certainly no longer despised, are still regarded as different. The Jews are still a peculiar people, and this should be the source of their greatest pride.

ISABELLA RENNIE

ABOVE Immigrants arriving in the new state

OPPOSITE ABOVE Druze villagers
celebrating the granting of religious
autonomy in 1961. The Druze, one of the
larger minority groups in Israel, are
members of a secret religion which broke
away from Islam in the 11th century

RIGHT June 1967: the Old City gates open
after the Six-Day War. Previously the
Old City of Jerusalem had been in
Jordanian hands

OPPOSITE BELOW Soldier on leave

At David's Tomb

Mount Zion is just twenty minutes' walk and only five minutes by car. There is a Greek Orthodox, a Catholic, a Protestant church or monastery (one of each) on Mount Zion. An Arab boy showed me the room where Jesus had his last supper. A perfect, elegant dining room in a beautiful old Arab house. In the courtyard looking down from the dining room on the first floor, to the left is the entrance to King David's tomb. The old bearded man sitting on a bench in the shade was already off duty and the night-watchman now in charge of the keys was 'somewhere around. But the place is closed, it's after 5.30 p.m. Come tomorrow.'

I was ready to wait. I wanted to see this tomb of the great king. I don't know what I expected from it. Two young, dark, local women with two small children had been here before me. They had come for a blessing: closed or not closed, with a bit of good will and maybe a small bakshish they would get in. Little did they know that this night-watchman was one of the very few saints in the world and probably the only one in Israel. He didn't want any money. He just wanted to go back to his room, three catacombs along the corridor, to start on his work. I didn't know it either until he took me back to his quarters. His duties at the tomb are to keep the keys at night, to switch lights on and off, keep the yard clean, occasionally talk to an angry inspector from the City Council (his employers) on the phone, but it didn't disturb him. Nothing disturbed him. He had no complaints. Josef is no Portnoy. Josef is not any Jew I had ever met before.

His reward for keeping the keys to the holy grail was the two hundred Israeli pounds a month and this place to sleep – a cool, damp catacomb, shielded from the rest of the cellars by a door made of wood, asbestos and corrugated roofing material. One door. No windows. Before Josef moved in it was a storeroom. Josef left

David's tower (LEFT), a landmark in the Old City of Jerusalem. BELOW is the archway known as David's Tomb

it that way, just making himself a small shelf for a teakettle, another shelf to write his books, and a third for his small Philips tape recorder and radio. From the two hundred Israeli pounds he has one hundred left at the end of the month. Nothing he could think of to spend his money on. His staple diet is leaves. 'You can eat all leaves, every single green leaf from trees, bushes, grass. Any green leaf, though some have more nourishment and taste better than others. I might one day maybe write this book on my diet, but that's too early. I'm still experimenting so to speak. Some leaves make me very ill and I lie here with cramps for a few days. But then the Highest puts me back on my feet again.'

Josef was small, had piercing blue eyes beneath excessive bushy eyebrows and a dark blond, slightly greying, scruffy beard. His black hat, instead of being dented in, pointed up. He wore an old dishevelled grey suit, a shirt that didn't fit him and shoes that were either too big or too heavy for him. On first sight I believed I had last seen him in the Gorky trilogy. He spoke Russian, Czech, German, Hungarian, Yiddish. My Yiddish is bad imitation. He didn't mind speaking German. He placed a few old broken chairs under an open bulb, offered me dried prunes and dried apricots and old boiled sweets from huge paper bags – and of course green leaves, which didn't taste too bad – and tea. We sat under the bulb like on an open stage and talked. He did most of the talking. I learned something from his 'turning point'. It happened at the end of the war when Josef, after a few days' march in an *Arbeits-kommando*, reached a casino occupied by the SS. Instead of shooting the Jews the commanding officer gave them a feast. The war was practically over and the SS men needed a few Jews for an alibi*.

Josef's turning point was also a day in March 1945. He owed his life to divine intervention and from then on devoted all his time to prayer and study and the writing of holy brochures which he printed at his own expense and sold to 'his customers' in town. The job as night-watchman at the tomb was his best deal in life yet. He said it left him with plenty of time to study and to write 'and what else is life all about but to praise the wonders of the Lord of the Universe, what else is there?' I can't think of anything else, either, Josef. This meeting with Josef at the tomb of David, this unique spot, was more than weird. As if I had found, exactly ten years later, the ending of the short novel I had started in the summer of 1961. I had expected anything to happen to it, but certainly not that.

JAKOV LIND

---

*Exactly this had been the story I wrote ten years before, *Soul of Wood*. The story is of one Anton Barth, who spent his war years in a forest where he survives miraculously as a deer among deer and is carried down from the wilderness into civilization by a few SS stragglers who are to capitulate to the Americans and need a Jew for an alibi.

The Diaspora Today

The proclamation of the state of Israel did not spell the beginning of the end of the Jewish presence in the wider world. While the great majority of Jews were proud that their homeland should be restored and recognized, many preferred to continue living in the countries in which they had made their homes. There they continued to experience the problems of a minority, how to maintain their independent existence as a people and a culture while finally taking their place as citizens of the lands in which they lived. The ways in which they have tackled these problems, and the extent to which they have been successful, have depended partly on their own strength and cohesion and partly on the extent to which they have been allowed by their host countries to realize their aims.

A Jewish tomb in Rome in the 1st century CE

Some 3,500 years ago a tribal leader living in Mesopotamia announced to his wife and family that they would be leaving home to move west across the Euphrates River. The people were not pleased with the decision of their leader, Abraham. They were loth to leave the land of their birth and their many kinsmen. Why would anyone want to migrate from Mesopotamia – at that time the most powerful empire in the world and a thriving centre of commerce and culture? What could be the attraction of the lands to the west – which seemed to offer only desert and wilderness?

On questions such as these the Hebrew nation enters the course of human history. It is appropriate that the origins of the Jewish people should be associated with questions which seem to defy logical explanations. For in the almost four millennia since Abraham decided to cross over the Euphrates, the history of his descendants has confounded those who have tried to understand it. Two major questions remain insufficiently accounted for by the usual rational approaches to man's history:

How has this people, in the face of persistent adversity, retained its historic continuity? How is it that such a numerically small group has had such a significant impact on the course of human history?

In the preceding chapters and stories, this book has tried to suggest some answers to these questions. The particular interest of this chapter is the Diaspora, the pattern of Jewish settlement inaugurated by that first journey. With Abraham's acceptance of the special mission for his people and with the designation of a particular land associated with that mission, the core elements of 3,500 years of Diaspora life are established.

The Diaspora Pattern

The history of a nation is typically written on its soil, where, over the course of time, the key events of its life are played out. Not so with the Jews. Their history has occurred in many diverse areas of the world. But there is a pattern to the diversity. It is represented in the two homelands known by Abraham. Just as he experienced the tension between Mesopotamia and the 'Promised Land', so too have generations of his descendants. Involved are two modes of settlement, one in Eretz Israel, seen as the authentic Jewish homeland (although for long periods it was not the home of the vast majority of Jews); and the second, those countless settlements of Jews in foreign countries, which are known collectively as the Diaspora.

Throughout Jewish history this pattern has persisted – simultaneous Jewish communities in the Holy Land and the Diaspora, with (after the destruction of the First Temple) a majority always living outside Eretz Israel. The area of the major Diaspora settlements has shifted over the course of time, with both the location and quality of the settlement largely a function of economic and political forces in the host nation. The adaptability of the Jew to the many diverse cultures in which he has lived has been noteworthy. He learned to speak the language of the country, fulfilled responsibly the civic duties expected of him, and sometimes fared well economically. The survival of the Jewish people can be accounted for in part by their adaptability, but it also stems from their determination to retain their separate identity wherever they lived, in spite of the severe difficulties this often entailed.

Although the Jews maintained themselves as a group apart, this did not mean that there was not a significant cultural exchange between them and their hosts. Over the course of time, many customs and ideas have been absorbed by the Jews from the non-Jewish societies in which they lived. Likewise, the Jewish presence has had an impact on the different cultures which have accommodated them.

In addition to the contact with the non-Jewish world, the evolving Jewish tradition has also been nourished by a second pattern of interaction – that between the Diaspora and Eretz Israel. Israel has always been viewed as the source of Jewish spiritual and national life. In one form or another, Diaspora Jews have always maintained links with Eretz Israel.

The word Diaspora comes from Greek and its literal meaning is a scattering of seeds. The most important pre-medieval Jewish settlements were in Babylon (now Iraq) and in Alexandria in Egypt. By the time of the Middle Ages the seeds of Abraham were widely dispersed in countries throughout the Middle East and Europe. They lived mainly under the influence of the two predominant civilizations of the period – Christianity and Islam. There

Night falls on the desert

was a clear distinction between the reactions of the Christians and Muslims to the Jews continuing to live in their midst. This differential reaction is the key to understanding the nature of Jewish life in the Diaspora communities during the Middle Ages.

That the Jews failed to accept the divinity of Jesus presented basic theological problems for the Christian. He responded by defining the Jew as an inferior being. His was an accursed race doomed to eternal exile. Thus the Jew had to be kept apart from the Christian and he was consigned to be a perpetual wanderer, without a land of his own – unless and until he accepted Jesus as the son of God. The Church through its laws and leaders lent its prestige to degrading and persecuting the Jew.

With such official sanction from the Church, it is not surprising that wherever Jews lived in Christian countries they were both feared and harassed by their neighbours (for examples, see 'The Martyrs', pp. 138–53). In such an oppressive atmosphere, physical survival alone was difficult. In spite of such conditions, however, the spiritual creativity of the Jews in medieval Christendom was striking.

A more hospitable climate existed for the Jews who lived in some countries under Muslim rule in South East Asia, Egypt, North Africa and Spain. While there were laws defining the Jew (and Christian) as a 'second-class' citizen, and curtailing his privileges, these were neither as harsh nor as systematically enforced as were the Christian regulations. In this more congenial atmosphere the Jews experienced a burst of population growth and intellectual expansion. Perhaps the acme of Jewish achievement took place in the medieval Jewish community in Spain, frequently identified as a 'Golden Age'.

For at least two centuries Muslims and Jews interacted with one another in a mutually productive relationship. Then Muslim Spain fell to Christian conquerors. Where Muslim political influence prevailed the earlier benevolent attitude towards the Jew was given up and replaced by more repressive policies. For both cultures the creativity of the Golden Age ended. Spain and several other Muslim countries came under Christian rule by the thirteenth century. Renewed activity to convert Jews to Christianity made the life of the Jew in Spain increasingly perilous. It reached its climax with the Inquisition and the expulsion of the Jews from Spain in 1492 and Portugal in 1497.

Types of Diaspora Communities

As the Jew stood on the threshold of the modern era, some 3,000 years after Abraham's journey, we can perceive some unique dimensions of his history. Contrary to the pattern of other nations, the history of the Jew was not bound with one geographic area.

In fact, the Jew maintained two homelands – one, Zion, which for many was largely spiritual, and the other, the Diaspora, involving many areas of the world, where much of Jewish life was lived.

Despite the many variations in Diaspora communities, we can categorize them into two types based on the style of response of the host country to their Jewish settlement: *benign* and *oppressive*. The former is best represented by the Diaspora communities in Babylonia and Muslim Spain; the latter by the settlements in the Christian nations of the Middle Ages. A reality common to both the benign and oppressive Diaspora communities is that the final frame of reference is the non-Jewish society. The degree of sovereignty that the Diaspora Jew has over his individual and collective life rests in the hands of the non-Jew. In the benign situation the Jew has access to the outside world, but this means he must measure and adapt his responses in the light of the prevailing non-Jewish values and culture. With freedom he is obliged to cope with the tension between separatism and integration. Further, decisions about the extent and duration of his free access rest fully with the non-Jew.

In the oppressive communities the degree of autonomy of the Jew is more clearly delimited. Where the oppression is interpreted mainly as restricted access to the non-Jewish world, intense creativity within the Jewish world has often been the result. Such a specifically Jewish development as the Yiddish culture of the eastern European *shtetl* was in large measure a response to exclusion from the gentile world. Confined physically and culturally in their encounters with the surrounding non-Jewish society, the eastern European Jews turned back to their own resources. The result was a flourishing authentic Jewish culture, secular and religious. However, when the gentile response to the Jew moved from being restrictive to oppressive, Jewish energies were deflected from creativity to survival. When the oppression was carried to its 'logical' extreme it produced the Holocaust and the destruction of the eastern European Jewish community.

That the destiny of the Jew in either type of community is profoundly affected by the non-Jew is confirmed by the frequent instances in history when a benign community is converted to an oppressive one. Witness the dramatic switch between the Golden Age of medieval Spain and Spain of the Inquisition, or the post-World War I Jewish community in Germany leading to the Nazi regime. Out of the ashes of this last, the most violent and extreme expression of anti-Semitism in history, arose the renewed Jewish homeland in Eretz Israel. The establishment of the State of Israel in 1948 marks the onset of the Third Commonwealth in Jewish life. Not since the time of the Roman conquest has there been a Jewish polity in the Holy Land. Two thousand years of Jewish hopes and prayers had been fulfilled. Would the exiles be ingathered from their widely scattered settlements? Would this mean finally the end of the Diaspora?

LEFT A bagel-seller in New York, the prototype 'benign' community

LEFT The ingathering of the exiles: Jews from the Yemen arriving in Israel

Percentage of the total Jewish population by continent in the mid-19th century, 1935 and 1973.
(The combined figure for Asia and Africa in the mid-19th century was 12%.)

SOURCES

Mid-19th century: Eban, Abba, *My People, The Story of the Jews,* Behrman House, New York, 1968.

1935 and 1973: *American Jewish Year Book,* American Jewish Committee, New York, 1936 and 1973.

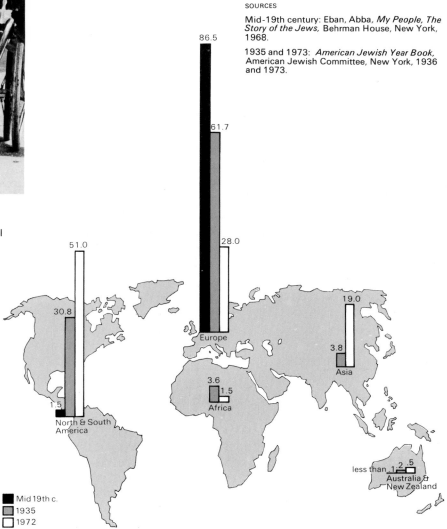

- ■ Mid 19th c.
- ▨ 1935
- ☐ 1972

The ten countries with the highest Jewish populations in 1935 and 1972.

SOURCES *American Jewish Year Book,* American Jewish Committee, New York, 1936 and 1973.

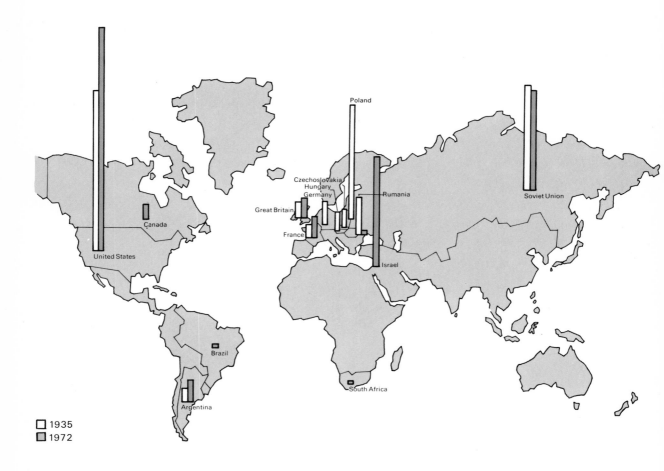

■ 1935
■ 1972

1935 Country	Population
U.S.	4,228,029
Poland	3,028,837
Soviet Union	2,778,548
Roumania	984,213
Germany	499,682
Hungary	444,567
Czechoslovakia	356,830
Great Britain	300,000
France	220,000
Argentina	215,000
Total Jewish Population	15,188,636

1972 Country	Population
U.S.	6,115,000
Israel	2,723,000
Soviet Union	2,648,000
France	550,000
Argentina	500,000
Great Britain	410,000
Canada	305,000
Brazil	150,000
South Africa	117,900
Roumania	90,000
Total Jewish Population	14,370,000

Estimated Jewish population in Arab countries in 1948 and 1973.

Of the approximately 50,000 Jews who today live in Arab lands, almost three-quarters are in Morocco. Many of those who remained are elderly. All are subject to severe restrictions. Following the Yom Kippur war in 1973, the situation grew worse, particularly in Syria, Egypt and Iraq, and the future status of Jews in these countries is uncertain. Mounting efforts have been launched to permit the remnants of the Jewish settlements in Arab countries to depart for lands where they can live without persecution.

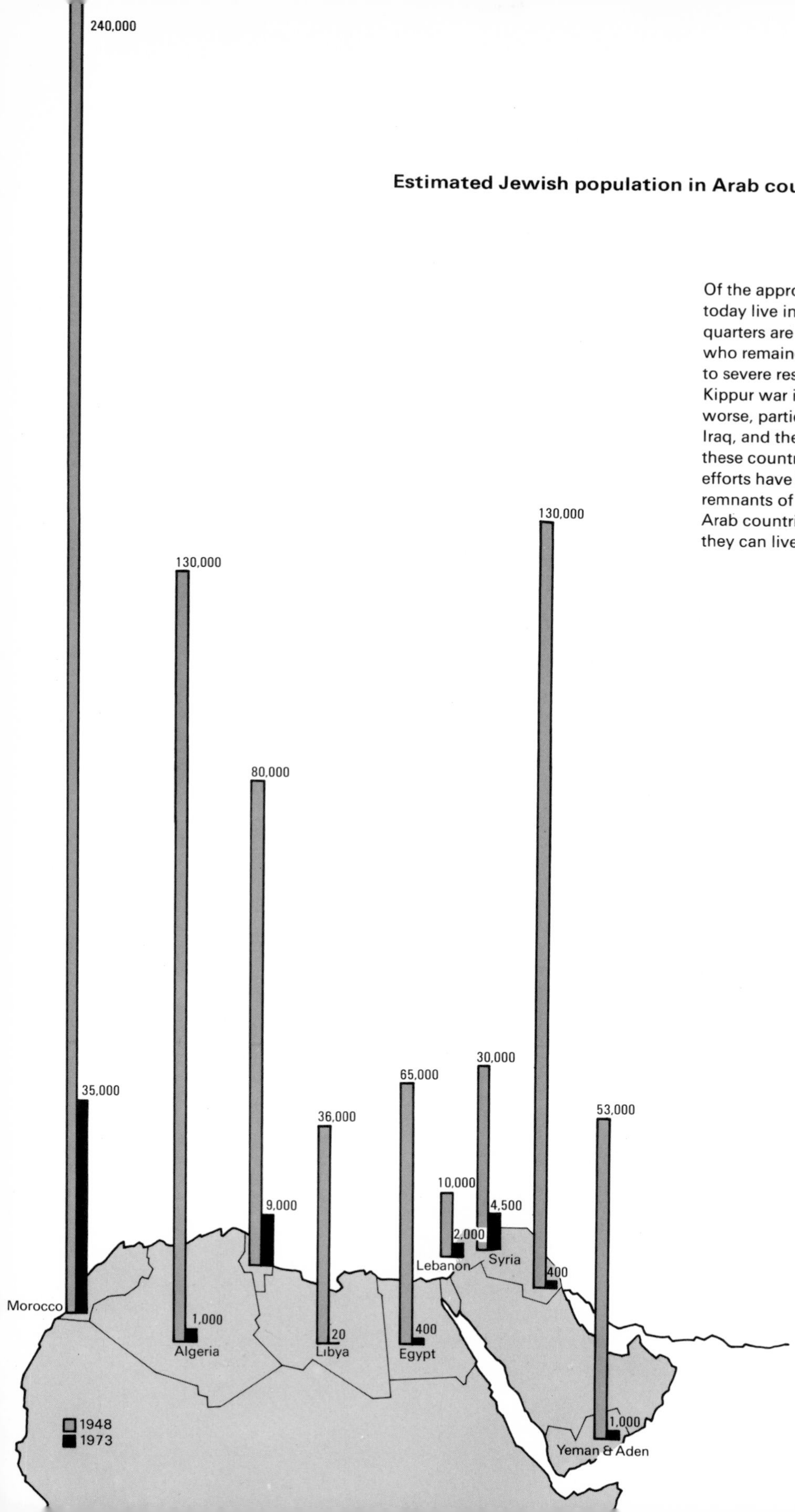

240,000

35,000

130,000

80,000

130,000

36,000

65,000

30,000

53,000

10,000

9,000

4,500

2,000

1,000

400

20

400

1,000

Morocco

Algeria

Libya

Egypt

Lebanon

Syria

Yeman & Aden

□ 1948
■ 1973

207

Demography of the Modern Jewish World

This brief historical review has highlighted the fact that the Jewish people has lived in a constant state of dispersal – sometimes by choice, more often because of adversity. Once more in the twentieth century the geographic distribution of Jews shifted.

In the middle of the nineteenth century 86·5 per cent of world Jewry lived in Europe (72 per cent lived in East Europe). Over the course of the next century, because of migration and the Holocaust, the Jewish population in Europe dropped to 28 per cent (see p. 205). During the same time the proportion of Jews living in America (most in the United States) grew from $1\frac{1}{2}$ per cent in the 1850s to 51 per cent in 1972. In 1850 there were 12,000 Jews living in Eretz Israel. By 1972 the Jewish population in Israel was the second largest in the world, comprising 19 per cent of the total Jewish population (see p. 206).

Eighty-one per cent of all Jews today live in the Diaspora and three out of four of these live in either the United States or the Soviet Union. The rest are scattered in 81 other countries throughout the world. In the following section we explore the current status and future prospects of Jews in the major Diaspora settlements.

The USSR

The Jewish community in the Soviet Union is in the tradition of the oppressed Diaspora communities of history. Except for a brief period soon after the Communist Revolution (1918), the Soviet Union has continued its country's characteristic policy of anti-Semitism. Like other minorities, the Jews of the Soviet Union are recognized as a nationality but not as a religion. Since the government controls the distribution of all economic resources, the effect of this policy has been to destroy the means of assuring Jewish continuity. No synagogues are built; rabbis, educators, religious functionaries are not trained; religious books and newspapers or ceremonial objects are not allowed or severely restricted. In addition, Jews have been singled out from other nationality groups for persecution and discrimination.

Harassed economically and socially, denied access to their religious culture and thereby unable to educate their young, it is truly amazing that after over fifty years of such treatment there has been a resurgence in Jewish identity in the Soviet Union. The first evidence of the renewed interest appeared in the 1960s when young people – most of whom thought of themselves as non-religious – appeared at synagogues on Jewish holidays. Increasingly, Russian Jews expressed their support for Israel, despite their government's growing hostility to Israel. Many began to study Hebrew, often in

OPPOSITE Hanukah lamp from 18th-century Germany

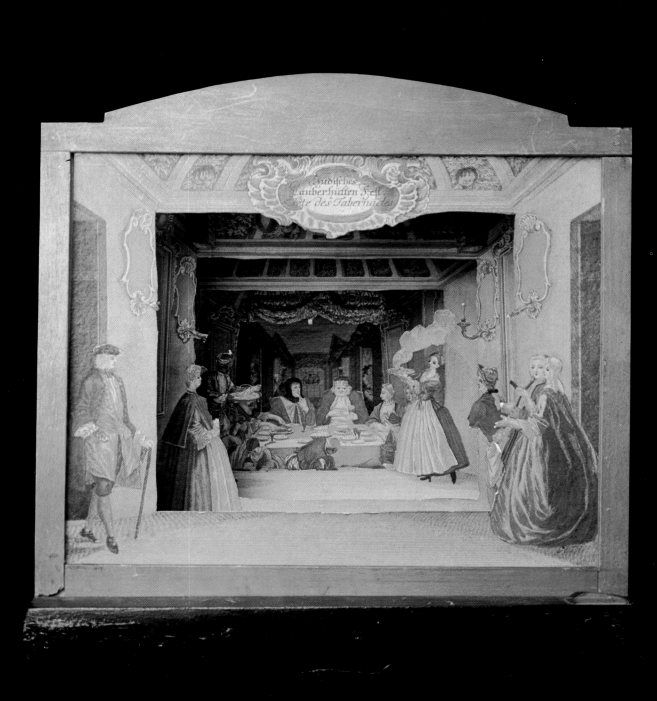

secret, in anticipation of a hoped-for emigration to Israel. In 1971 and 1972 a total of 44,000 Russian Jews migrated to Israel. The emigration figure for 1974 was 20,000. These combined figures represent less than 3 per cent of the Russian Jewish population. How many others want to migrate? Will the Soviet government permit continuing migration? Will the Jews who remain in the Soviet Union be willing or able to sustain a Jewish community without access to religious or cultural institutions and trained leadership? The answers to all of these questions rests with the Russian government. Its historical record does not give cause for optimism.

Jews in Arab Countries

Since the destruction of the First Temple in 586 BCE, Jews have lived in the lands of the Middle East and North Africa. The Jewish communities in Arab countries thus precede the establishment of Muslim rule in the eighth century CE. While historically Jews experienced varying degrees of harassment and restrictions in all Muslim countries, they lived for centuries in some of these lands in a relatively benign society. The situation deteriorated rapidly with the spread of German influence in the Middle East just before and during World War II, and changed drastically with the establishment of the state of Israel in 1948. In most of the Arab countries anti-Jewish activity became rampant, with resulting destruction of Jewish lives and property. Ancient synagogues were destroyed, Jewish property and institutions were confiscated, and the limited civil rights of Jews were further severely curtailed. As a result, a mass exodus of Jews began, with the vast majority of emigrants settling in Israel. Jewish communities, some of which had existed for 2,000 years, virtually came to an end (see p. 207).

The United States

The Jewish community in the United States is the epitome of the benign Diaspora type. Within America's hospitable shores has emerged the largest Jewish settlement in Jewish history.

Jews in the United States have reached an unparalleled degree of success in their achievements and influence. They are better educated and have higher incomes than the average American. U.S. Jews play a significant role in the cultural and intellectual life of the country. They are active in the communications industry, the literary world, the theatre, and in the universities. Although less than 3 per cent of the population, they comprise over 10 per cent of all American college teachers. Anti-Semitism has never been a major problem in the United States and what earlier evidences of discrimination existed have now been virtually eliminated.

OPPOSITE Child's toy from 18th-century England, a peep-show with a *sukkah* inside

The two largest Diaspora communities: USA and USSR

OPPOSITE ABOVE Moscow Central Synagogue, a showcase of Soviet 'toleration'

OPPOSITE BELOW LEFT One who escaped. After having been imprisoned for Zionism, Tina Brodetskaya was finally allowed to leave the USSR in 1970. Here she wears the number which identified her in a Soviet 'special camp'

BOTTOM CENTRE Jewish Women's Lib conference in the USA

BELOW 'You are not forgotten'. A demonstration on behalf of Soviet Jewry at the Western Wall, Jerusalem

BOTTOM RIGHT American Jewish students in a Soviet Jewry solidarity march

An assertion of Black Power at the Olympic Games, 1973. Black Power led to many forms of ethnic renaissance, including that of Jewish groups

In recent years there has been evidence of a resurgence of interest and activity in the areas of Jewish culture and religion. The American Jewish community has always had an extended network of Jewish social welfare institutions. Currently the trend is to clarify and upgrade the Jewish components of the services and leadership of these institutions.

The renaissance in Jewish life is particularly striking among young Jews. Disenchanted with the cathedral-like synagogues to which they were heir, they have generated a score of *havurot* – a new form for Jewish communal worship, study, and living. On the college campuses – where Jewish students once commonly chose to escape their heritage – the interest in Jewish learning has led to the development of a number of formal programmes of Jewish Studies as well as voluntary Free Universities. The growth of Yeshivoth and Jewish day schools since World War II has been remarkable.

How is this renewed interest in Jewish identity in the United States to be explained? Most would agree that its genesis could be traced to the late 1960s. A critical turning point was the Six-Day War (1967). The awareness that the future existence of Israel was in jeopardy brought to consciousness all the latent memories of the Holocaust. The American Jew (as well as most other Diaspora Jews) realized that his fate was intertwined with that of his fellow Jews. The subsequent decisive victory of the Israelis added to a sense of reawakened group pride and loyalty.

Also occurring in the latter half of the 1960s was the Black Revolution, an event which had an important impact on American Jews. In the first instance Jews were caught short when they found themselves not only rejected as allies by the Blacks, but also frequently the object of their hostility. For Jews, it was the opening of a breach in their identification with the liberal movement. The disenchantment with the liberal camp grew as many of their former allies directed their support to the Arabs in the Arab-Israel conflict. Finally, the newly affirmed pride of the Blacks resulted in a general ethnic renaissance in America. The melting-pot concept, an ideal to which earlier generations of Jews and other American immigrant groups had subscribed, was now supplanted by the notion of cultural pluralism. Highlighting one's ethnic origins, whether Italian, Irish, Polish, Black, or Jewish, was now in vogue in the United States.

The diversity of expression in Jewish communal life in America is unparalleled. It includes a full gamut of denominational activity – Reform, Conservative, Orthodox and Reconstructionist, each accompanied by its panoply of organizational structures, plus many variations, such as active Hasidic communities, Yiddishists, Zionists, and a large secular Jewish population identified with an extensive network of charitable and fraternal organizations.

But the American-Jewish scene is not without its darker side.

Despite a post-World War II boom in synagogue building, only approximately one-half of all American Jews are affiliated with a synagogue, and the rate of participation in religious services is the lowest of the major religious faiths in America.

Cultural continuity depends in large measure on how the next generation is educated. The effectiveness of the Jewish educational system in the United States has been seriously questioned. One out of every five Jewish youths is not involved in any formal sustained programme of Jewish education. Of those who receive a Jewish education, almost half attend schools which meet only one day a week.

Great concern has been focused on the problem of intermarriage. Based on figures produced in a recently completed National Jewish Population Study, the evidence on the scope of the problem is mixed. The national figures indicate an increase in the rate of intermarriage, but not of the order suggested by earlier more limited studies. Of all Jews currently married, 9·2 per cent are intermarried. This compares to a figure of between 6 and 7 per cent in the period between World War II and the 1960s. Nearly half of the original non-Jewish mates subsequently identify themselves as Jewish, although less than a quarter undergo formal conversion. Although there may be a gap between intent and actual behaviour, the figures on religious identification of the non-Jewish mate and the plans for rearing children suggest that the loss to the Jewish population through intermarriage is less than the rate would lead one to expect.

The American Jewish community, based on its accomplishments in American society and the tangible evidences of Jewish communal life (structures, organizations and money raised), has the earmarks of an outstanding community. Viewed from the perspective of the quality of its Jewish communal life the verdict is less clear. The range of options for Jewish living is impressive, although these options are not always firmly rooted in the Jewish heritage. Recent stirrings in the Jewish community give hope to the prospects for a revitalization of its religious and cultural life. To the extent that this occurs it will confirm that the Jewish community in America has become one of the great civilizations in Jewish history. It will further confirm that it is possible to sustain a viable Diaspora community in the post-Emancipation age.

Great Britain

Outside the United States, the major benign Diaspora settlements are to be found in the English-speaking countries of the British Commonwealth. Of these countries Great Britain has the largest Jewish population (410,000) and its generally sympathetic response to its Jews has in large measure shaped the response of the other

Henry Kissinger, US Secretary of State

MARKS' PENNY BAZAAR

ANY ARTICLE 1^D

Commonwealth countries. The history of the Jews of Great Britain typifies how the pattern of Diaspora Jewish life varies in response to major themes of its host country. A small Jewish community existed in England during the twelfth and thirteenth centuries and was expelled in 1290. In the sixteenth and seventeenth centuries, descendants of Conversos who had fled to Holland from the clutches of the Inquisition in Spain and Portugal gradually settled in England, where they were known as 'Portuguese merchants'. Wishing to attract such vigorous and prosperous people from Holland, Britain's main trading rival, Oliver Cromwell tacitly permitted Jews to return to Britain after 1656. Numbers grew gradually, and the early arrivals were mainly Sephardim. The mass immigration of Ashkenazim from eastern Europe increased the Jewish population from 65,000 in 1880 to 300,000 in 1914.

The progressive social policies of Great Britain afforded British Jews a level of civic and political rights beyond that of most European nations. During the nineteenth century, the Anglo-Jewish community achieved an important position of influence both in English society and as a spokesman for world Jewry. During the Damascus Affair of 1840, when Jews in Syria were

persecuted, it was Sir Moses Montefiore, a leader of the Anglo-Jewish community, with the support of the British government, who interceded.

Many current developments in the Jewish community of Great Britain parallel those of the Jewish community in America. British Jews have fared well economically, a high percentage of their children attended university, and they are moving from their city neighbourhoods to suburban areas. Living in an open society with little anti-Semitism, British Jews are concerned with the problem of assimilation. Studies indicate that the rate of intermarriage ranges from 12 to 25 per cent. The population loss due to intermarriage, a birth rate which is lower than the general population, plus an annual rate of *aliyah* to Israel of between 1,000 to 2,000 has resulted in a Jewish population which has not grown in the past decade.

A unique feature of British Jewish life is the centralization of religious authority in the position of the Chief Rabbi. In other European countries the *kehillah* was the organizing force for the Jewish community; in Britain Jewish communities centred around the synagogue. The Chief Rabbinate emerged to provide a coordinating force for the national Jewish community. It also paralleled the centralized religious authority in the Anglican Church – the Archbishop of Canterbury. The current Chief Rabbi, Immanuel Jakobovits, was appointed in 1966. Like his predecessors, he is an Orthodox Jew. A majority of British Jews are identified with either of several Orthodox groups – the United Synagogue (a federation of London area synagogues headed by the Chief Rabbi) and the smaller Federation of Synagogues and Union of Orthodox Synagogues. Reform and Liberal Jews comprise about 10 per cent of the population. The figure of those non-affiliated with synagogues is estimated at between 25 and 30 per cent. All sectors of the community come together in their positive commitment to Israel and support for Jews in the Soviet Union.

Other Diaspora Countries

The future of most other Diaspora countries is much more dependent on Israel than is the case with those described above. One major exception is France, the only European country to which Jews have migrated in fairly large numbers since 1945. About 50 per cent of the Jews who fled North Africa in the 1960s settled in France. In the main French Jewry is well integrated, while retaining a flourishing cultural identity, although De Gaulle's anti-Jewish speech after the Six-Day War gave a boost to *aliyah*. In almost all other Diaspora countries the proportion of their population which goes on *aliyah* is high. Frequently those who leave on *aliyah* are the most committed of the Jews of the country, thus draining potential leadership. The smaller Diaspora communities

ABOVE Lord Lionel Rothschild, to whom the Balfour Declaration, promising a National Home for the Jews in Palestine, was addressed in 1917

OPPOSITE ABOVE The beginning of Marks and Spencer, the most widely known Jewish enterprise in Britain

OPPOSITE BELOW Jewish welfare organizations in Britain, as elsewhere, care for old people as well as children

also suffer from the lack of adequate institutional resources to train an indigenous corps of Jewish professionals. It is difficult to convince a new generation of, for example, Brazilians, Australians, Italians, or Argentinians that there is a serious Jewish future in their country when so many of their teachers, rabbis and youth leaders are from Israel or the United States.

The question is whether a Diaspora community can sustain itself when its existence is based primarily on an identification with Israel. In the short run, Israel serves to inspire the Jewish commitment of the Diaspora communities, but without other nourishment – particularly among young people – it leads to decisions to settle in Israel rather than to assume leadership roles in their native countries.

Many of the small Diaspora settlements are in countries which lack a stable government, and a continuing source of insecurity for these settlements is the possibility that the next regime may be less sympathetic to its Jews. There have been numerous instances in modern history where a country that has maintained a friendly attitude to its Jewish population has made a sudden, dramatic turn-about.

Claude Lévi-Strauss, world famous anthropologist, who was born in Belgium and teaches in France

The Future of Israel and the Diaspora

Traditionally Jews describe the 2,000 years of Jewish history between the destruction of the second Temple and the establishment of the State of Israel as *Galut* (exile). This is in distinction to the term Diaspora, which implies a voluntary settlement. It is a state of *Galut* even if the person lives of his own choice outside his homeland since living in a non-Jewish environment the Jew cannot know his spiritual and cultural fulfilment and thus is inevitably alienated. Yet today, more than a quarter of a century after the Jewish state was born, the great majority of Jews continue to live in the Diaspora. Aside from some Jews in the Soviet Union and the small numbers still in Arab countries, they remain voluntarily. Will Jews in the era of the newly established Third Commonwealth continue to maintain the Diaspora, and if so, will the Diaspora communities reflect and contribute to the Jewish historical experience?

A view held by some Jews is that inevitably, and appropriately, Jewish life outside Israel will disappear. David Ben Gurion expressed a pessimistic outlook on the Diaspora in the book *Jewish Heritage* (1973): 'There can be no such thing as Jewish culture in the Diaspora . . . the non-Jewish surroundings are dominant, their influence is felt in the economy, the law, the language. Specifically Jewish life, insofar as it exists, is compressed into a small corner without roots in the reality surrounding it.' It is only in Israel, Ben Gurion contends, that 'one can be a complete person and a complete Jew'.

Dr Albert Sabin, US bio-chemist

For others the Diaspora is seen as an integral part of the Jewish historical experience and one which will continue, along with Israel, to play a vital role in the future of Jewish life. What is required is to define a relationship between Israel and the Diaspora which will contribute most to the enrichment of the Jewish experience. One approach, conceived by Ahad Ha-Am, sees Israel as the spiritual centre of the Jewish universe:

[The] dispersion must remain a permanent feature of our life, which it is beyond our power to eliminate, and therefore it insists that our national life in the Diaspora must be strengthened. But that object . . . can be attained only by the creation of a fixed centre for our national life in the land of its birth . . . which can exert a 'pull' on all of them, and so transform the scattered atoms into a single entity with a definite and self-subsistent character of its own. (*The Jewish State and the Jewish Problem*, 1897.)

An alternative definition of the relationship between Israel and the Diaspora was outlined by Simon Rawidowicz, who saw Jewish life as having two centres: Israel and the Diaspora.

It is not only as an extension of the Jewish historical experience that the existence of a strong Diaspora is important, but also

ABOVE Bob Dylan, most acclaimed of all folk singers

ABOVE RIGHT Barbara Streisand, singer and comedy actress

OPPOSITE Leonard Bernstein, conductor and composer

RIGHT Mark Spitz, US Olympic swimmer and frequent gold medallist

because the joint presence and interaction of Israel and the Diaspora will make more likely the fulfilment of the Jewish destiny. This means the survival of the Jewish people as a distinct entity. The review of Jewish history in this book has highlighted two constant themes: Jewish survival in the face of persistent adversity, and the significant impact this numerically small people has had on the course of human events. The key is distinctiveness – Jews have survived because they acted and believed differently from the multitudes. At the same time it was as a result of their distinctiveness that their creative contributions to society have emerged. By being an evident minority the Jew has invariably occupied the status of an outsider. His interaction with the majority was characterized by a tension – a tension which was converted into Jewish creativity, both to the advantage of the majority and to the Jew. In the first instance the interaction with the diverse societies led to a mutually productive cultural exchange. Secondly, the contrast reminded the Jew of his difference and led him to delve more deeply into his own sources so as to understand and clarify his existence.

The interaction between the Jewish communities of Israel and the Diaspora in the contemporary world can enhance the authentic Jewish survival of both. At the most obvious level this means the sharing of material, political and cultural resources as needed by each community. But there is also the critical corrective role that Israel and the Diaspora can play for one another in assuring that they remain true to their Jewish distinctiveness.

Israel is not without threats to its Jewish continuity. We have been so focused on the physical threats to Israel's survival that less attention has been addressed to the matter of the State's Jewish essence. Here the process of 'normalization' could lead to a dulling of the traditional Jewish sensibilities to social injustice. Similarly, out of the pressures of building a national state arises the danger of a situation in which there are diminishing conscious links to other Jews and to the Jewish historical experience and in which Jewish religious expression becomes marginal. The interaction with the Diaspora can help keep these incipient trends from deflecting Israel from its basic Jewish purposes.

When Abraham led the Jewish people into history he was responding to a Covenant with God. That Covenant has inspired his descendants for almost four millennia and in many diverse locations. In the future, we can expect that Covenant will continue to inspire the Jewish people, whether they live in Israel or the Diaspora. For, as Abraham Heschel has said: 'God is no less here than there. It is the sacred moment in which His presence is disclosed. We meet God in time rather than space.' (*Israel: an echo of eternity*, 1969.)

BERNARD REISMAN

Glossary

Where a term is itself defined elsewhere in the glossary it is set in capitals.

Aggadah (Hebrew, 'narrative'), those portions of the TALMUD and MIDRASH which contain legends, stories, folklore and expositions of the Bible.

Aliyah (Hebrew, 'going up'), emigration to Israel.

Amora, plural *amoraim* (Aramaic), the Jewish scholars of the 3rd to 6th centuries CE living in ERETZ ISRAEL and Babylonia whose discussions and rulings on the MISHNAH formed that part of the TALMUD known as the GEMARA.

Aramaic, an ancient language, related to Hebrew, which was commonly spoken in ERETZ ISRAEL and Babylonia from around the 3rd to 11th century CE.

Ashkenazim (Hebrew), heirs to a Jewish culture which spread from northern France and Germany in the Middle Ages to Slavonic countries and thence all over the world. The common language of the Ashkenazim was Yiddish. Their traditions were distinguished, as early as the 14th century, from those of the SEPHARDIM. Today the main Ashkenazi centres outside Israel are the USA and USSR.

Byzantine empire, the Christian empire of the East, which lasted from 330 CE until the fall of Constantinople to the Turks in 1453.

Conversos (from Latin), Jews of Spain and Portugal, and their descendants, who had been converted to Christianity, generally by force. They are sometimes also called MARRANOS.

Diaspora (from Greek), the Jewish settlements outside ERETZ ISRAEL.

Ein Sof (Hebrew, 'without end', 'the Infinite'), the name used in Jewish mysticism, the KABBALAH, for God in His essential being.

Eretz Israel (Hebrew), the biblical name for the Land of Israel. After the fall of the Second Temple in 70 CE, it was used to mean the Promised Land. From the end of World War I (1918) until 1948 it was the official Hebrew name for Palestine as governed by the British mandatory authorities.

Essenes (origin uncertain), Jewish religious brotherhood which practised a communal and ascetic way of life. Their communities, which flourished from the 2nd century BCE to the end of the first century CE, were mainly established along the north-western shores of the Dead Sea.

Galut (Hebrew), the exile of the Jewish people from ERETZ ISRAEL.

Haganah (Hebrew), the officially secret armed Jewish defence force organized in Eretz Israel during the British Mandate. It later formed the basis of the Israeli army.

Halakhah (Hebrew), those portions of the TALMUD which deal with Jewish law, and rabbinical decisions which have been accepted as binding.

Halutz (Hebrew), 'pioneer'. One of the early Zionist groups was called He-Halutz, 'the pioneer'.

Hasidism (Hebrew *hasid*, 'pious'), a Jewish revivalist movement with its roots in mysticism and popular piety which originated in Eastern Europe in the first half of the 18th century. Its followers are known as Hasidim.

Heder (Hebrew, 'room'), a school where young children are taught Jewish religious observances.

Irgun (short for Hebrew *Irgun Tsvai Leumi*, 'National Military Organization'), initially a break-away group of HAGANAH, established in 1931. Rejecting Haganah policy of restraint, the Irgun engaged in armed reprisals against the Arabs and later in active attacks on the

British authorities. A splinter group of the Irgun, founded in 1940 by Avraham Stern, assassinated Lord Moyne in Cairo in 1944. Bitterness between former Irgun and Haganah members continued to be a feature of Israeli politics after independence.

Kabbalah (Hebrew), the name generally used for the Jewish mystical tradition. Students of Kabbalah are called kabbalists.

Kaddish (Aramaic, 'holy'), the prayers and congregational responses recited at the close of sections of the public service in the synagogue and at the end of the service itself. A special *kaddish* is recited by mourners, close relatives of the deceased.

Kehillah (Hebrew), the Jewish congregation.

Ketubbah (Hebrew), the marriage contract on which a husband records the financial obligations he undertakes in respect of his wife.

Kiddush (Hebrew, 'sanctification'), the prayers said over wine and bread on the evenings of Sabbath and Festivals.

Marranos (origin unknown), a term used scornfully to describe those Jews of Spain and Portugal who were converted to Christianity but continued to practise Judaism in secret. Jews who had similarly been coerced into becoming Muslims were known as *Jadid al-Islam*.

Midrash (Hebrew), collections of rabbinical interpretations of Scripture.

Minhag, plural *minhagim* (Hebrew), customs, either those accepted as binding by the whole Jewish community, or those belonging to a particular locality only.

Minyan (Hebrew), the ten adult males necessary for communal prayer according to Jewish Law.

Mishnah (Hebrew), the earliest code of Jewish oral law, written in Hebrew and arranged by Judah ha-Nasi at the beginning of the 3rd century CE.

Mitzvah, plural *mitzvot* (Hebrew), a biblical or rabbinical commandment or religious duty. The word is also commonly used to mean a good deed. *Bar-mitzvah* means literally 'a son of the commandment(s)'.

Pogrom (Russian), an attack by one section of the population on another. It is specifically used for the attacks on Jews in Russia between 1881 and 1921, which were sanctioned by the authorities. These pogroms stimulated the wholesale emigration of Jews, particularly to the USA, and contributed greatly to the rise of Jewish nationalist feeling and the Zionist movement.

Sasanids (from Sasan, a Persian proper name), the ruling dynasty of the Persian empire from 211 to 651 CE. During part of this time, their empire included ERETZ ISRAEL.

Sefirot (Hebrew), a mystical term for the ten spheres which are stages in the manifestation of EIN SOF. Each one is an aspect of God.

Sephardim (Hebrew), descendants of the Jews who were expelled from Spain and Portugal in 1492. Their culture and customs are somewhat different from those of the ASHKENAZIM and for centuries they continued to speak a form of Spanish known as Ladino. Like Yiddish, Ladino is now dying out.

Shekhinah (Hebrew, literally 'dwelling'), the Presence of God, which encompasses the people of Israel. In KABBALAH the *Shekhinah* is the feminine principle in the mystical world of the SEFIROT.

Shtetl (Yiddish, 'little town'), Jewish settlement in Eastern Europe, of a type which originated in Poland in the 16th century and came to an end, also in Poland, with the Nazi occupation.

Siddur (Hebrew), daily prayer book.

Takkanah, plural *takkanot* (Hebrew), a regulation issued by the scholars of the HALAKHAH which is binding on the Jewish community. These enactments were issued at times and in places which enjoyed a considerable measure of self-government.

Tallit (Hebrew), the prayer shawl worn by males, usually after marriage, often after *bar mitzvah*. It is customarily white, fringed, and has black or blue stripes woven into it.

Talmud (Hebrew, 'learning'), the body of interpretations and elaborations of the MISHNAH put forward by the scholars of ERETZ ISRAEL and Babylonia, from the 3rd to the 5th centuries CE. Two differing compilations exist, known as the Babylonian Talmud and the Jerusalem Talmud. Both are written in ARAMAIC, though in different dialects. The Babylonian Talmud, the later one, became widely accepted as authoritative. Until emancipation, the Talmud was the major source of Jewish education.

Tanna, plural *tannaim* (Aramaic), word first used in the TALMUD for Jewish scholars of the first and 2nd centuries CE. The later authorities are called AMORAIM.

Tefillin (Hebrew), two black leather boxes containing passages from Scripture which are bound, by leather straps, on the forehead and left hand for the weekday morning services. The word is usually, and incorrectly, translated into English as 'phylacteries'. The Teffillin are worn by males who are over the age of *bar mitzvah*.

Zohar (Hebrew, '(Book of) Splendour'), the major book Bible, often used loosely for the whole Bible; also the entire body of traditional Jewish law.

Tzaddik (Hebrew, 'righteous man'), used especially for a Hasidic rabbi or leader (see HASIDISM).

Zohar (Hebrew, '(Book of) Splendour'), the major book of Jewish mysticism (KABBALAH), written in both Hebrew and ARAMAIC.

Illustration Notes and Acknowledgments

Page numbers set in **bold type** refer to the pages opposite the relevant colour plates. Where two numbers are given in **bold type** this refers to the double-spread colour plate between the two pages.

Temple Israel

Minneapolis, Minnesota

In Honor of the Bar Mitzvah of
MICHAEL ALAN ROZMAN
by Parents,
Delores & Bennie Rozman

January 10, 1981